Project Retrospectives

A HANDBOOK FOR TEAM REVIEWS

Project Retrospectives

A HANDBOOK FOR TEAM REVIEWS

NORMAN L. KERTH
foreword by GERALD M. WEINBERG

DORSET HOUSE PUBLISHING
353 WEST 12TH STREET
NEW YORK, NEW YORK 10014

Library of Congress Cataloging-in-Publication Data

Kerth, Norman L.
  Project retrospectives : a handbook for team reviews / Norman L. Kerth
    p. cm.
  ISBN 0-932633-44-7 (pbk.)
    1. Computer software--Development--Handbooks, manuals, etc. I. Title

QA76.76.D47 K48 2001
005.1'068'4--dc21

                                                            2001017250

Cover and Interior Illustrations: Rich Terdoslavich
Cover Design: David W. McClintock

Distributed in the English language in Singapore, the Philippines, and Southeast Asia by Alkem Company (S) Pte. Ltd., Singapore; in the English language in India, Bangladesh, Sri Lanka, Nepal, and Mauritius by Prism Books Pvt., Ltd., Bangalore, India; and in the English language in Japan by Toppan Co., Ltd., Tokyo, Japan.

Printed in the United States of America

Library of Congress Catalog Number: 2001017250

ISBN: 0-932633-44-7   12   11   10   9   8   7   6   5   4   3   2   1

Acknowledgments

I started work on this book believing that authors are solo practitioners who struggle by themselves through the various trials of content, discovery, format, grammar, invention, and English. Along the way, I discovered that books are not the effort of a lone author but involve the generous and selfless help of so many people. I'd like to name all those precious people who helped me make this book possible, but it is probable that I will thank everyone except that one most important person, whom I now stupidly seem to have forgotten. If you are that person, please know that I'll remember your name ten minutes after this work has gone to press, and that you and your contributions are no less appreciated than those listed here.

Who are these people who helped make this book possible? They include the following:

Don Reifer, the man who introduced me to the ritual of a retrospective.

Tom DeMarco, who simply sent an e-mail asking me what I knew about holding retrospectives—Tom, here is my answer.

The participants in my retrospectives, the students in my courses, and the numerous people who have e-mailed me about their retrospective experiences—you helped me to refine my understanding of the ritual and to discover what is important to say and how to say it.

My colleagues and fellow facilitators, who generously shared their ideas and experiences over the many years. I have, no doubt, taken your ideas, incorporated them into my work, and forgotten your individual contributions, but I have not forgotten your importance to me—III, Eileen Andreason, Peter de Jager, Bob King, Jim Batterson, Jinny Batterson, Michael Dedolph, Naomi Karten, Phyllis Kramer, Mark Manduke, Ian McIver, Judah Mogilensky, Judy Noe, Bill Pardee, Pat Sciacca, Shel Siegel, Pat Snipp, Tom Solano, Linda Wensrich, Eldonna Williamson, Rebecca Winant, Kay Wise, Johanna Rothman, Karl Wiegers, Ellen Gottesdiener, Eileen Strider, James Bach, Dani Weinberg, Jean McLendon, Karen Straka, Steve Smith, Bruce Hobbs, Bent Adsersen, Frank Sisti, Hugh Gratz, Bunny Duhl, Andy Streich, Mike Ginn, and Wayne Bailey.

The people who read my early writing, took a course, or participated in a retrospective, and then found the courage to lead one themselves: Brian Batke, Sue Bartholomew, Bradley Kerth, Ron Jeffries, Roger Kelly, Amy Schwab, Janis Aaron Moore, Michael Green, Jeanine Brown, James Henry, Tom Hawes, Bob Connoly, Kirt Loerke, Colleen Rinehart, Beth Schmitz, and Ron Thompson.

The reviewers of this manuscript, many of whom are master retrospective facilitators in their own right: Diana Larson, Linda Rising, Dan Starr, James Tierney, John Graves, Mary Lynn Manns, Payson Hall, Shauna Gonzales, Martin Fowler, Luke Hohmann, Brian Lawrence, John Rae-Grant, Wayne Strider, David Schmaltz, Esther Derby, and Maureen O'Hara.

Anne Jacko, whose masterful editing greatly improved an early draft of this work; the many talented people at Dorset House Publishing but especially Nuno Andrade, Wendy Eakin, and Matt McDonald, whose unflagging encouragement and editorial guidance have exceeded my highest expectations; and Rich Terdoslavich, whose illustrations translated my ideas for cartoons into true masterpieces. Thank you all.

My parents, Ruth and Roy Kerth, who instilled a core belief in me when I was young that I relied on many times while writing and rewriting. You taught me to believe that you can achieve anything your heart desires and you can accomplish anything you set your mind to.

Steve Lawrence, friend and fellow struggling author, who understood the importance of being able to compare notes as we each developed our own manuscripts.

Peggy Doherty, who shares so many facets of my life. Thank you for the many times you said, "Norm, you have to finish your book," as I considered accepting yet another consulting opportunity. Your encouragement for me to keep writing as we watched our savings dwindle was truly remarkable.

Finally, Jerry Weinberg, who helped me understand *the way of an author* through his countless e-mails, discussions, gentle nudging, and encouragement. Yours was a most generous gift.

I am blessed and thankful to have each of you in my life.

DEDICATION

To those great managers,
So interested in brightening their skills,
That they fought for a way to hold a retrospective,
While conquering their fears of what they might find.

Contents

Foreword

I've been looking forward to Norm Kerth's book since I first learned he was writing it. I need it for my consulting practice. My clients need it for their process improvement programs. The software industry needs it in order to become truly professional. And nobody in the world knows more about project retrospectives than Norm.

To me, retrospectives are primarily about learning. Without information about past performance, there can be no learning. Though this essential role of feedback is a basic principle of psychology, it doesn't yet seem widely understood or practiced in the software industry.

Feedback is built into many processes in life, especially those by which one attempts to manipulate the physical world. If I try to thread a needle, for example, I can tell immediately whether or not I have succeeded. Same with kicking a field goal or building a wall—but not so with software. We in the software industry are working with a more or less invisible product, yet this very invisibility only heightens our need for feedback. We aren't going to get feedback implicitly, so we have to build it explicitly into our processes—hence, our need for retrospectives.

Feedback on software projects—meaningful feedback, at least—is not easy to come by. Projects often outlive the accuracy of our memories. Even when our memories are excellent, people leave during the project and take their memories away with them. So, in order to capture project learnings, we need to plan, prepare, and practice. And that's what *Project Retrospectives: A Handbook for Team Reviews* gives us—plans, preparations, and practice.

Retrospectives, of course, are human cooperative processes—calling on qualities that are not typically the engineer's strongest. One of the best features of Norm's book is how it speaks to an engineering audience in engineering terms, teaching us how to transform what we know about software engineering into *social engineering*.

Another strong feature is the book's attention to issues that are sometimes considered peripheral to the retrospective itself—activities such as selling the idea of retrospectives, qualifying the potential customer, obtaining and maintaining support, creating a community, coping with legal issues, thinking in advance about the what and how of data capture, and even considering such details as what kind of food to serve during the retrospective, and when.

Project Retrospectives is a strong book, full of strong features that will make it the classic work in this area. In my opinion, though, the very strongest feature of the book is its many well-designed exercises—exercises that will elevate your chance of success—whether you are a new or experienced facilitator of retrospectives.

As I wrote at the outset, I've been looking forward to this book. It was worth the wait.

January 2001   Gerald M. Weinberg
Albuquerque, New Mexico

Preface

Here is Edward Bear, coming downstairs now, bump, bump, bump, bump, on the back of his head, behind Christopher Robin. It is, as far as he knows, the only way of coming downstairs, but sometimes he feels that there really is another way, if only he could stop bumping for a moment and think of it.

—A.A. Milne, *Winnie-the-Pooh*. London: Puffin Books, 1926.

So begins A.A. Milne's children's classic *Winnie-the-Pooh*. In these opening lines, Milne invites us to identify with the predicament of Edward Bear: The usual way of doing things—the routine—is not necessarily the best way and it is certainly not the only way. As I read Milne's words, I marvel at the parallel between the world Milne describes and our own crazy world of software development. As software developers, we bump our heads in project after project, day after day. If we would only take a moment to stop and think of alternative ways to proceed, I'm sure we could find better ways to do our work.

Project Retrospectives: A Handbook for Team Reviews details creating a special ritual at the end of each project that lets us stop and reflect before proceeding with the next project. This ritual, called by many names—postmortem or postpartum, for example, or, my preference, retrospective—is important to our practice of software. In fact, I believe that it is the single *most important* step toward improving the software process! The reason for this is that a well-run retrospective can help members of a community understand the need for improvement, and motivate them to change how they go about their work. The community designs the changes, since it knows best how to identify, organize, and give priority to the problems to be solved. Owning the changes helps the community become the master of its software process. The process is the community's—to use, to honor, to modify, or to discard. Most important, it is the community's to review, again and again, after each project.

A retrospective can also help facilitate process improvement and changes that involve more than one team. The changes are often complex and cross group lines, requiring cooperation between multiple teams. A retrospective helps build this cooperation. The practice of holding retrospectives also serves as the cornerstone for efforts to improve software process. Given the rapid speed at which the software development field changes, we need to continually revise our work practices. Retrospectives assure that the software process adapts to advances in the field.

If a project fails, holding a retrospective provides a way for project members to learn from the failure and move beyond it. Its structure helps team members discuss how to improve, without eliciting accusations of blame or implications of shame. By avoiding a review of a failed project, the community loses a valuable opportunity to learn from its experience, possibly leaving the door open for the same kind of failure to happen again.

However, a retrospective is not just about improving software process. It also fosters learning, growth, and maturity in the participants. It provides an opportunity for project members to celebrate the successes and acknowledge the heroes in their community. The stories shared in a retrospective become part of a group's tribal knowledge and tradition, as well as a source of long-term learning for the community. The experiences recalled during a retrospective help build a team with a common focus.

A retrospective can deliver on all these promises, but only if it is managed well. Learning to lead a retrospective isn't exceptionally difficult, but how to do it best is not always an obvious process. It is my goal in *Project Retrospectives* to help you become a skilled retrospective facilitator, enabling you to provide the best possible experience for the software community you are leading as well as for yourself.

October 2000   N.L.K.
Portland, Oregon

Project Retrospectives

A HANDBOOK FOR TEAM REVIEWS

CHAPTER ONE

Introduction to Retrospectives

There once were three little pigs who, after surviving numerous harrowing encounters with the Big Bad Wolf, lived happily in their sturdy brick house at the edge of the forest. Having ousted the wolf, the pigs once again felt safe in their neighborhood. One day, the pigs decided to venture into the forest to visit their friend Owl. They liked Owl because he was very wise and could entertain them with all sorts of stories.

The story Owl told on this day entailed a group of humans and their repeated failed attempts to drain a swamp. The humans couldn't complete the job because they kept running into alligators. After listening to the story, the pigs questioned why the humans needed to deal with the swamp in the first place. "Don't these humans know," the littlest pig asked Owl, "that swamps can be avoided altogether if they get Beaver and his crew to build dams to control water flow?"

"Don't humans learn?" wondered the biggest of the three pigs. "Why don't they learn to build dams?"

Owl replied, "It is a kind of insanity humans have. Humans, as a species, have hope. They hope that even if they do things that didn't succeed before, that by doing them the same way twice, they will get different results."

The pigs laughed with delight, and exclaimed, "Humans are the silliest creatures!"

Owl merely nodded, and then, having finished his story, he asked the pigs how their new project was going. "Great," they replied. "Unlike those humans, we learned a valuable lesson from our last project." The pigs told Owl how they had tried straw and twigs but had found brick to be the best building material they had ever used. They believed it would serve them well again for their current job— one on which they would build a real-life-tested structure to withstand even the strongest winds. In fact, the pigs explained, they would never use straw or branches to build anything again.

When the visit was over, Owl watched the pigs leave. He doubted that Noah, their client, would like the brick ark the pigs were building for him.

Engineering software means dealing with project alligators of all kinds while striving to remember what the true goal is. The three pigs wonder why one experience in the swamp is not enough to cause the humans to stop and question the premise for their activity—in other words, to ask why they are in the swamp in the first place.

Owl is wise, but the pigs do not share his wisdom—the *learning* that comes from experience. Without this type of learning, most creatures are in danger of reliving earlier experiences—landing back in the swamp time after time.

The three pigs believe that they have learned from their experience building wolf-proof homes, but have they acquired real wisdom? In a time of crisis, they select the first workable solution without careful analysis of its strengths and weaknesses or of its application to the present circumstances. Instead, they believe that what worked so well in one situation is the perfect technology to use in all their engineering efforts, whether they are building a house or an ark.

The pigs, like so many of us in the software engineering field, are missing the *bigger picture*. They are not adept at selecting the appropriate technology for the specific project at hand. Their amused reaction to the foolish behavior of the humans in Owl's story gives credence to a fundamental observation about how all living creatures learn. I call this The Law of Wisdom Acquisition:

It is much easier to identify another's foolishness than to recognize one's own.

This law suggests that it is not natural for us to stop, reflect, and learn from our software projects. Of course, this is true! I am usually worn out at the end of one of my alligator-infested swamp-draining projects. I have hundreds of e-mail messages to deal with, a stack of journals I need to catch up on, and all sorts of other business issues that I have let slide. More importantly are the personal issues: I have to reconnect with my family and friends, start my exercise program again, and prepare for my postponed vacation. I might finally have time to go to the dentist, get my car serviced, buy some new clothes, and so on.

The act of reflecting on my just-finished project is not naturally a high priority. Yet it is the key to ensuring that my next project will have less water to drain and fewer alligators to manage.

The Need for Ritual

Since stopping to reflect on a project is not a natural activity, one must formalize the behavior and make it a ritual. Rituals serve to bring people together, helping them to focus on what's important, and helping them to acknowledge significant events or accomplishments.

The end of a software project is an ideal time for a ritual that helps people to reflect and be retrospective. The word "retrospective" itself means *looking back on, contemplating, or directed to the past*. Such a retrospective ritual should lead us to reflect on our project and allow us to look at our mistakes and learn from them.

But a retrospective ritual should not focus only on our mistakes—to do so misses so much! Every project has success stories that need to be heard and heroes that need to be honored. We learn things during a project, and we need to acknowledge what we learned or risk forgetting it. Therefore, the end of a project is also an excellent time to capture and analyze useful metrics—real numbers that can be used in the scheduling of future activities.

A retrospective ritual needs to include the entire community. Such a ritual can bring about a great deal of learning, and should not be limited to just a few individuals. It should involve everyone associated with the project. One person cannot know the whole story of the project; one individual's reflection can only bring about small-picture learning. While one person might learn from specific experiences—like handling alligators with extra-long tails or sloshing water over a dike—there won't be big-picture learning—such as how to keep alligators from entering the swamp, how to prevent the formation of a swamp in the first place, or how a certain way of sloshing water gets in the way of the people on the other side of the dike.

This big-picture wisdom comes from our ability to understand the relationship between an individual's work and that of the entire team. We need to tell our piece and see how it helps make up the whole story. As a retrospective facilitator, I have seen whole-team reflection explain, discover, and teach so much. I believe that there is no better way to improve a team's performance and quality.

Retrospective rituals are more than just a review of the past. They also provide a chance to look forward, to plot the next project, and to plan explicitly what will be approached differently next time.

NAMING THE PROCESS

In the software industry, retrospectives go by many names. One popular term is *postmortem*, from the Latin for "after death." While this term has been widely used, I don't favor it since it suggests that looking back on a software project is like examining a dead body! Software projects don't, or at least aren't supposed to, end with death; rather, they bring something to life. As an alternative, the Latin term *post partum*, meaning "after birth," is sometimes used—but it is a term I have ceased to use because the term is frequently associated with the depression some mothers experience after giving birth. I have discovered that people who have had difficulty during childbirth associate the term *postpartum* with pain and may have memories that are likely to interfere with the review process.

A client of mine told me that throughout his career in the U.S. Army, he participated in a *Post Engagement Redress (PER)* after every major event in which he had been involved. By making a few calls to friends in the military, I learned more names for this ritual. The Army also uses the term *After Action Review (AAR)*. The U.S. Navy uses *Navy Lessons Learned (NLL)*, and sometimes even calls the review a *Hot Wash Up*. The U.S. Coast Guard has a great acronym: *C-GULL (Coast Guard Uniform Lessons Learned)*.

While all these terms have their own appeal, I never grew comfortable with any of them. Then, Wayne and Eileen Strider, two fellow facilitators, suggested that we call what we do a *retrospective*. The word seemed appropriate; it didn't carry any loaded meanings and it could be applied to projects without implication of success or failure. So far, this word has served me well.

PRIME DIRECTIVE FOR A RETROSPECTIVE

For a retrospective to be effective and successful, it needs to be safe. By "safe," I mean that the participants must feel secure within their community—to discuss their work, to admit that there may have been better ways to perform the work, and to learn from the retrospective exercise itself. *Safety* must be developed and maintained. While safety is ultimately the responsibility of all the participants in a retrospective, the facilitator needs to initiate, monitor, and control the safety. Part of being safe means knowing that there will be no retribution for being honest (such as being given a negative evaluation during the next performance review). Trust must be established and maintained during a retrospective.

In an ideal world, this kind of safety and trust would be a natural way of doing work. In the real world, members of the community may feel only a small degree of safety or trust. Each participant needs to choose the level of safety that is right for him or her. A method for expressing "unsafe" ideas during the retrospective needs to be established. To begin building safety and trust, the facilitator must communicate the prime directive for *all* retrospective rituals:

> **Kerth's Prime Directive:**
>
> **Regardless of what we discover, we must understand and truly believe that everyone did the best job he or she could, given what was known at the time, his or her skills and abilities, the resources available, and the situation at hand.**

This directive, which I consider fundamental to my approach, reflects a mindset that needs to be part of everything that happens before, during, and after a retrospective ritual. As long as participants reflect this attitude, safety and trust can exist, and the retrospective can be a productive learning experience. If the prime directive is violated, the possibility of a successful retrospective ritual is significantly diminished and the retrospective will fail.

THE DARKER SIDE OF RETROSPECTIVES

Negative experiences with retrospective rituals can be disastrous. Sue Christila, a colleague of mine, wrote the following to me:

> . . . most of the <retrospective rituals> that I have been involved with seem to have had the common flaw of turning into complaint sessions rather than learning sessions and, by virtue of that, the information wasn't necessarily highly regarded (if not disregarded) and didn't seem to be incorporated into subsequent projects.

Sue's experience is not uncommon. Poorly run retrospectives can easily become gripe sessions, and when they do, very little can be learned.

Complaint energy is tricky to handle. The message in the complaint is worth listening to, but the packaging of the complaint can harm the learning process. Usually, the person issuing the complaint

- has only a partial understanding of the circumstances
- has experienced negative results from the project
- has developed a negative attitude through hindsight
- is feeling disempowered

The author of a complaint usually is not aware of the harm done by how he or she presents the message—such a person sees that there is something to be conveyed but doesn't realize that the listener is put off by the complaint itself. Negative packaging is the first thing the recipient of the complaint sees, and this will probably prevent him or her from extracting the real message.

In the worst cases, when complaint energy is taken to an extreme, retrospective gatherings can become hostile. Individuals who are singled out for blame and fault during retrospectives often stop listening and can no longer learn. The following is an excerpt from an e-mail I received from one individual who was the victim of outright destructive hostility:

> . . . the attacks started slowly. The first was small and tentative. I made the mistake of partially agreeing and partially defending myself. I was trying to learn and to acknowledge that I was not perfect. I was accused of being defensive and not listening. Funny, but I believe that I was the only one in the room who was really listening.
>
> Anyway, by mid-day I was being attacked for almost everything, even if I had nothing to do with the situation. The side conversations at lunch and breaks were enough for me to close down and stop participating. Because of this experience and the following day-to-day interaction with my peers, I quit four months later.
>
> After a decade, I still carry the trauma from that meeting. I'm not sure I would enter into another <retrospective ritual>.
>
> I believe what happened was that people did not feel safe to look at their faults and, as a result, diverted the meeting away from themselves by attacking me.
>
> My metaphor for that <retrospective> is one of twenty sharks feeding on a carcass.

Under such negative conditions, retrospectives cannot be expected to communicate any wisdom to participants other than "Don't attend a retrospective!" One problem that was apparent from the above story was that no one felt safe enough to discuss faults.

A way to deal with complaints at a retrospective ritual is simply to outlaw them, but this is a bad idea. Complaints are based on valid experiences that need to be examined; they are the clues that there is an underlying problem awaiting discovery. In the design of a retrospective ritual, we need to use activities that will dissipate complaint energy and help us learn from complaints without letting their energy become destructive.

THE RETROSPECTIVE FACILITATOR

An important element in the retrospective process is its leader, called a facilitator. To learn to lead requires careful training and study. The retrospective ritual's form, activities, and goals develop over time and are continuously refined. To learn to lead a ritual, a novice needs to acquire wisdom passed down from experienced leaders.

Becoming a facilitator for a software retrospective ritual involves much more than just helping people get together to talk about the project. What it does involve is the subject of this book, which is written for people who are committed to becoming retrospective facilitators. I expect that by reading this book, you will be introduced to many new concepts and ideas. One reading will adequately prepare you to plan small-scale retrospectives, but, with practice, you'll learn how to become a master at facilitating retrospective rituals. Start with small projects, in which team members have worked well together. With time, try larger projects and consider teaming up with a more experienced facilitator to learn how to handle a retrospective for a community that has strong feelings about the project.

This book can be read as an overview of the topic by those who want to learn about retrospective rituals, or as a handbook for facilitators to use when planning and running a retrospective ritual. If you are reading this book to get an overview, you probably will want to look at the overview sections carefully (Chapters 2 and 3) and then browse through the more technical, exercise sections (especially those in Chapters 6 and 8). If you already are a facilitator, then all the techniques discussed in Chapters 3 through 10 will help you to plan and hold a retrospective. Since every project and every team is different from any other, every retrospective needs to be different as well. There is no one right way to lead a retrospective. You will need to take the ideas in this book and tailor them to your style of facilitating. Because one topic may lead to other reference material, a facilitator may decide to seek training outside the software-engineering field. This guidebook is meant to start the process by describing the steps needed to take a reader into the world of facilitation.

During my years as a facilitator, people have asked me to provide a set of step-by-step instructions on how to run a retrospective. I generally respond that I can't draw a map because I've never been to the terrain that they are about to enter—

remember, every project is different! However, I can provide instructions that can be used as guidelines. Readers can use this book as a guide to traversing unexplored terrain. Armed with this guide, readers can combine its wisdom with their own wits to survive the new wilderness of a retrospective ritual.

CHAPTER TWO

Anatomy of a Retrospective: A Case Study

If you have never participated in a successful retrospective, then it may be hard to imagine what one is like by simply reading a book. To help you visualize the process, I have put together a brief case study in the following pages to give you a sense of what can and should occur in a well-run retrospective. The chapter contains an overview of many of the topics and discussions that will be developed further in later chapters, tied here into a single story. The story is based on an actual retrospective, but I've spiced it up with bits and pieces from other retrospectives to make it a more comprehensive composite.

The chapter introduces a battery of exercises and tools that I use in retrospectives, most of which will be discussed more fully in later chapters of the book. You will see that the example does not make use of all of the possible exercises—for the simple reason that I never use all the exercises in any single real-life retrospective—but it does show how I deviate from an existing plan as the occasion calls for it.

THE SAMPLE RETROSPECTIVE

The retrospective on which this case study is based was intended to review a project that produced complex software to help the genetic-engineering community predict results of a commercial gene-splicing effort. The team was very strong in domain knowledge. Of the two-dozen team members, seventeen were genetic engineers who had learned programming skills as a requirement to complete their doctoral degrees. Their only shared programming language was FORTRAN. The group also included four software developers who knew little about gene-splicing but had expertise in developing UNIX-based applications. The remaining three members of the team were managers who had led the project. Although 24 people made up the original project team, one manager and two of the genetic engineers were out sick for the duration of the three-day retrospective, leaving a core group of 21 participants to review the project.

Prior to working on this project, this group had been part of a research environment. The team had not produced a software product before. During the project, problems abounded: The project missed the schedule for several delivery dates; late in the project, major sections of code had to be thrown away and rebuilt from scratch; staff stability suffered as several key genetic engineers abandoned the project to take early retirement; and everyone who remained was grossly overworked throughout the final number of months.

The project was critical to the research unit's future as company management wanted to change the unit from a research center to a revenue-generating product-development center, stating it was tired of funding research for research's own sake.

The product, about 400,000 lines of code, eventually shipped about six months late. The system had defects in it, but they were not serious enough to prevent its acceptance in an emerging market. Customer response was positive, but few sales resulted.

PREPARING FOR THE RETROSPECTIVE

As part of my preparation for holding the retrospective, I interviewed each of the participants. I came away with the following impressions, which are listed loosely in cause-and-effect order:

- The managers were nervous about participating in the retrospective. They saw it as an evaluation of their ability to manage, and they feared it would show that they had not yet learned how to be good managers.
- The software developers were reluctant to participate because they were completely worn out and discouraged. They felt badly that they had missed the original schedule by six months, but they felt worse about the impact the project had on their personal lives.
- The managers were frustrated by the fact that letting individuals "do their own thing" during the schedule slips (as had been the norm in the research environment) had resulted in production of system components that would not integrate.
- The lead manager, who had taken on the role of systems architect and had directed the genetic engineers to develop specific components, was hostile to the genetic engineers who had resisted this change, which they viewed as a loss of scientific freedom.
- The software developers were angry at the managers for shifting into a micro-manage mode late in the development process. The developers felt they were being treated unprofessionally, and they believed that the managers should have set the general direction and then trusted the developers to do their job.

On the whole, I sensed that team members had very little pride in what had been accomplished. Everyone was focused on what had gone wrong, and could not see what had gone right. Before starting the three-day retrospective itself, I made it clear that the retrospective was not to be a finger-pointing or blaming session, but rather an opportunity for the participants to learn how to improve. I explained that a retrospective is much like an archaeological dig, and asked the participants to search for meaningful artifacts from the project to bring into the retro-spective.

THE RETROSPECTIVE PLAN

I always enter a retrospective with a plan that reflects my best guess of what the group needs to resolve. My plans have a beginning, a middle, and an end. However, as sessions unfold, I usually find that I need to adjust my original plan, discarding some ideas and adding others. For this retrospective, I planned as follows:

Beginning

My Goals:

- Help the community to get comfortable with me and with the idea of reviewing the project.
- Help participants create an environment in which they can articulate what is most important to them.
- Help participants realize that this project was a success because, although the odds were against them, they shipped a product.

My Approach:

- Select exercises appropriate to the specific situation. For example:
   "Define Success" Exercise
   "Create Safety" Exercise
   "Artifacts Contest" Exercise

Middle

My Goals:

- Review the project for significant learnings.
- Repair damage to working relationships between team members.
- Recognize the costs of producing such a great volume of work.

My Approach:

- Select exercises appropriate to the middle of a retrospective. For example:
  "Develop a Time Line" Exercise
  "Mining the Time Line for Gold" Activity
  "Passive Analogy" Exercise
  "Repair Damage Through Play" Exercise

End

My Goals:

- Determine what long-term activities need to occur for the next project to be more successful.
- Identify what alternate group behaviors need to be accepted now that the group is to be less research-oriented and more product-oriented.

My Approach:

- Choose closing exercises. For example:
  "Cross-Affinity Teams" Exercise
  "Making the Magic Happen" Exercise

Because flexibility is important to the success of a retrospective, I do not attach a well-defined or rigid schedule to a retrospective plan. In this sample, allocating times would have been difficult since I didn't know how the group dynamics would develop. I trusted my skills as a facilitator to make sure we would cover this plan in three days; otherwise, I would need to revise the plan based on the events that occurred. The following sections reflect how the events were handled. (Note: In this case study, I've used italics as a convention to highlight first use of the names of exercises so readers can locate them easily. The convention is not used elsewhere in the book.)

RETROSPECTIVE DAY 1

Beginning (Morning, Day 1)

Right before the opening meeting, the division head decided that he would attend the kick-off session. He wanted to tell the group how important he thought its work was. I believe he was also curious to see what went on in a retrospective. After thinking about how I could take advantage of the division head's presence, I decided to put more emphasis on understanding what had been accomplished, and elected the *"Define Success" Exercise*.

Once the division head had completed his pep talk, I asked group members whether they themselves thought the project was a success. Some members offered half-hearted self-congratulations, but they seemed unconvinced, and so I stopped the discussion.

To show team members how to quantify the success, I presented the results of an effort data analysis I had asked one of the team members to prepare prior to the start of the retrospective. We looked at the total number of lines of code, the number of lines per defect, the number of lines produced per day, and so on. I then contrasted what they had accomplished with software industry norms. I talked about the odds against a 400,000-line program ever being delivered, based on industry history, and pointed out that their success in completing the project put them in the top few percent of their field. From one point of view, they were very successful. Everyone seemed to be stunned by this fact, including the division head. I let this sink in.

Then I suggested another measure of success, saying, "At the end of a successful project, everybody says, 'Gee, I wish we could do it again.' Using this standard, was the project a success?" The group admitted that it had not been this kind of project, and stated that it would be great if we could figure out how to achieve this. I asked if anyone had ever been on such a project and a few people had, so I asked those individuals to talk about what their experience had been like. This discussion allowed us to explore how we could create such a project next time. With people's spirits significantly lifted, the division head departed, and I returned to my original plan. I repeated my statement that the retrospective process is not aimed at finding fault, but at learning how to do something better the next time.

I then introduced the *"Create Safety" Exercise.* I emphasized the fact that participation in individual exercises is optional. Everyone agreed to this basic rule, including the managers.

Since there were managers in the room, I wondered out loud whether people felt it would be safe to say what needed to be said. To find out, I had group members use secret ballots to show how safe they felt. Two people indicated that they did not feel very safe at this point in the session.

I then asked the participants to move into natural-affinity groups—groups made up of people who have a close working relationship—and directed the managers to form their own affinity group. The remaining team members divided into one group of genetic engineers and one group of software developers. Next, I charged each of the three natural-affinity groups with finding a private space in which to develop ideas that would increase the level of safety. After about half an hour, I called the groups back together and asked them each to report their ideas. This reporting session was followed by a discussion of how best to integrate each idea into the retrospective. One important request was for a session without managers, at which non-managers could meet privately. I agreed that I would report the results of the non-manager session to the managers, who could then ask questions about the outcome of the session.

We also established the following ground rules for group behavior:

- We will try not to interrupt.
- We will accept everyone's opinion without judgment.

- We will talk from our own perspective, and not speak for anyone else.
- There will be no jokes made at the expense of anyone in the room.

Despite our ground rules, a number of individuals in the group found it difficult to participate. A few people would speak so quickly after someone else's comments that others didn't get an opportunity to speak. One manager suggested that we design the exercises so that everyone *must* speak. The manager's intentions were good—he wanted to encourage quieter individuals to participate—but forcing people to speak violated the retrospective's rule that participation is optional, a rule based on the premise that when people are *forced* to say something, they are likely to say what they think management wants to hear, rather than what they really believe. After some discussion, we decided we needed some tool or object to signify a speaker's right to speak without interruption. A manager volunteered his coffee mug as a speaking tool, and we agreed that if a person had something to say but was unable to get the group's attention, he or she could pick up the mug. At that signal, everyone else was to stop talking and listen until the mug was either put down or passed to another person. We added the following ground rule to our list:

- If someone is holding the designated coffee mug, then only that person may speak.

The ground rule prohibiting people from making jokes about other people in the retrospective is one I always establish. Sometimes, humor can be used to communicate endearment, but sometimes it is used to humiliate. As a facilitator from outside the organization, I can't always tell the difference. Furthermore, there may be times when someone in the retrospective is feeling vulnerable and even gentle kidding might be taken as an insult. I have found it best to suspend all individual-based humor.

Once the group guidelines had been set, it was time to survey group members again to determine how safe they now felt. The second set of ballots showed that everyone felt comfortable enough to move on to the next activity: the *"Artifacts Contest" Exercise.*

A week prior to the retrospective, I had asked prospective attendees to become high-tech archaeologists and search their offices for important artifacts related to the project. At the retrospective, as part of the "Search for Artifacts" Exercise, I asked people to present and describe their artifacts, telling the story behind their treasures. We placed the artifacts on the floor in the middle of a circle of chairs. We studied what each attendee had brought, discussed the importance of each selection, and then voted for the most significant artifact from the project and for the most unusual one. We also determined who had brought the largest collection. Many of the artifacts from this particular project were documents. Someone even had a collection of all the schedules, including the first one prepared for the project. Everyone in the group laughed at how naive they all had been. Another document described coding standards that many in the group had fought to implement, only to have no one use. One important artifact was a place mat from a pizza parlor on which someone had sketched a new design for the database. When implemented, this revision had increased performance eightfold.

One engineer brought in a can of Raid bug killer. The can had appeared on his desk the day after he spent the night on systems integration and debugging and had uncovered several serious bugs that had plagued the group for weeks. I asked him what this can of insecticide meant to him. He explained that when he found the can, there had been a note attached to it that just read, "Thanks." He didn't know who had given the can and note to him, but it meant a lot that a co-worker had appreciated his effort. After he finished his explanation, someone commented, "Well, I didn't give you that can, but I do want to say, you did good." Others in the group agreed, and then suddenly, the whole group applauded him. I'll remember the smile on his face for a long time.

As time passed, the pile of artifacts grew into a remarkable collection. From the discussion of the artifacts, everyone could understand how much really had been accomplished during the project.

As I looked around the group, I concluded that we had achieved the goals for the beginning of the retrospective and were now ready to move on to the middle of the plan. As it was nearly noon, we broke for lunch.

Middle (Afternoon, Day 1)

When we reconvened, I initiated the "Develop a Time Line" Exercise. In this exercise, each participant adds details to a story recounting the project, contributing pieces to a collective history. This activity is designed to help group members remember everything that occurred during the project.

To start things off, I passed out five- by eight-inch index cards to the three natural-affinity groups, and gave each group its own color of marker pen. I then sent each group off to a private space where group members could identify significant project events or happenings, listing one event per card. (By assembling people in natural-affinity teams, I expected to reduce the number of duplicated cards.) I instructed the groups to make this an inclusive, rather than consensus, activity. That is, any member of the group who thought an event was important could create a card for it. (I always find it interesting to see how different natural-affinity teams view the same event from different perspectives, and to see which events are not widely appreciated by all the groups.)

While the groups worked on their cards, I taped butcher's paper to the wall, marking it according to seasons. When the groups were done with the cards, we taped them to the butcher's paper, positioning each card in the section marked for the season in which the event took place. The result was a time line of the whole project that showed what project members viewed as the significant events. Once this card-taping activity was completed, everyone stood back and observed, noting how the cards told the story of the project from many different perspectives.

With dinner-time approaching, I knew we wouldn't have enough time to process the time line, so I altered my original plan and rescheduled time-line processing for the following day. In its stead, I selected a different exercise to finish the afternoon session: the "Offer Appreciations" Exercise.

After observing that people in the group had seemed genuinely impressed when they looked closely at all that had gone into finishing their project, I told the group that the remaining time was a good opportunity to discuss that feeling. I explained the "Offer Appreciations" Exercise and started it off by voicing an appreciation of my own.

First, I complimented the genetic engineer who had developed and installed the project's configuration-management and change-control systems. This particular engineer did not have any specific training in the area of configuration management, but had taken it on faith that it was important. I stated that his effort was one key to the project's success. I then asked him to offer appreciation for someone else's work.

Appreciations continued to be traded until one of the managers took his turn, and completely took over. Feeling frustrated because I was letting each person offer only one appreciation at a time, he said he needed more than one turn. He then proceeded to give everyone in the group a sincere and significant appreciation. For some members of the group, this was the first time they realized that this manager even knew what they had done. I could see that team members were beginning to feel better about each other and to pull closer together as more appreciations were offered.

Although I had planned to run a *"Passive Analogy" Exercise* that night, I sensed that the team would get more out of doing something recreational. We ended the session by deciding that we should head over the hills to a winery a few miles away. So, off we went, spending the evening comparing wines and wine labels, debating the importance of the color of a wine bottle and of cork versus plastic stoppers, and discussing the difficulties and joys of making wine.

RETROSPECTIVE DAY 2

Middle (Morning, Day 2)

I started the second day by asking, "How did last night's activity resemble the project we are reviewing? How was it different?"

I wasn't looking for a specific answer, but wanted people to think about their interaction on the project in contrast to how they had functioned in a purely recreational setting. Of the many interesting observations, the one that seemed most insightful came from one of the genetic engineers: "Well, last night's outing was like what we used to do all the time when we were a research organization. But then we got too serious about making a product and we lost sight of how to have fun." Silence followed that comment as the group reflected on it. In order to allow people more time to consider the comment's implications, we agreed to table further discussion in favor of moving on to analyzing the time line in the *"Mining the Time Line for Gold"* activity—part of the "Develop a Time Line" Exercise.

Taking the time line season by season, we looked at events to see what we could learn. During the remainder of the morning, we worked through the whole project, identifying what was effective, what lessons were learned, what could be done differently next time, and what topics needed more detailed study.

When we broke for lunch, I allotted enough time so that everyone could eat and then get outside for some recreation before we resumed with the next session. A few people went for a walk, others talked as they tossed Frisbees, and another group played touch football on the tennis court. Although I didn't explain this to the group, by interspersing work sessions with recreation, I hoped to keep energy levels high.

Middle (Afternoon, Day 2)

For the post-lunch time slot, I asked the managers to go off to first discuss what they had heard so far and then to develop a brief message summarizing what they would like the genetic engineers and software developers to think about. With the managers gone, I began the *"Session Without Managers"* Exercise, working with the team of engineers and programmers to develop a message for their managers.

Because the people wanting a session without managers may be feeling powerless, small, and vulnerable, this exercise is tricky to lead. When people feel this way, they may develop an angry, blameful, or more subtly negative message. I helped the group to form a message that was honest without being accusatory.

As the lone facilitator on this retrospective, I could only interact with one of the groups at any given time. Left to their own devices, some management teams develop inappropriate messages, but fortunately, this particular management group did not. If I had known in advance that we would need to break into one group of managers and one of non-managers, I would have arranged to have a colleague work with the management team. Instead, I read what the managers wrote before they presented it to the other participants and saw that it was fine. (If I had believed there to be a problem, I would have arranged to delay their message until after dinner so that I could work with them through dinner to redirect or rephrase the message.)

After dinner, the managers and developers reunited into a single team. I presented the developers' message to the managers, giving the managers a chance to respond before they delivered

27

their own message. Discussions were getting pretty honest by this time.

I was struck by the similarity of the messages, despite their having been prepared from different points of view. This does not always happen.

Middle (Evening, Day 2)

I ended the day with the *"Repair Damage Through Play" Exercise* by staging a friendly competition between natural-affinity groups in games of pool, Ping Pong, air hockey, and pinball. I explained that the group to win the most points would get a trophy. I had brought with me an old trophy I had found at Goodwill that I'd had inscribed with "1st Place—Retrospective Extracurricular Activities." The trophy looked hokey, which was the effect I wanted.

RETROSPECTIVE DAY 3

End (Morning, Day 3)

When we reconvened the next morning, we reviewed, organized, and listed in order of priority the topics that needed more detailed study from the previous day's "Mining the Time Line for Gold" activity. These topics often turn out to be politically loaded, involving intense interactions between natural-affinity groups. On the previous day, when the goal was to view the whole project, I chose not to address these difficult issues, reserving the final day as the right time to analyze problems and propose solutions.

Working as one large group, we reviewed the ordered list, and blended and merged some items. Next, to begin the *"Cross-Affinity Teams" Exercise*, I split the group of non-managers into teams composed of a mixture of members from each natural-affinity group. I then divided the full list of problems evenly among what were now *cross*-affinity teams (teams made up of people who did not generally work together), and sent the teams off to study their assigned problems from multiple perspectives. Teams were instructed to take two hours to look for possible solutions and to develop a proposal for management to review. Managers made themselves available either as consultants or, if invited, as members of a cross-affinity team. After approximately two hours, I reassembled the community and asked individual teams to deliver their preliminary reports to management. Armed with feedback from the larger group, the teams then returned to their small cross-affinity groups, working until the lunch break to prepare final reports for management. As a bonding strategy, I urged each cross-affinity group to eat together and then to go for a walk. By encouraging such close group interaction and by keeping members together for the walk, I hoped to foster the kind of major breakthroughs in problem-solving that should occur during a retrospective's third day.

End (Afternoon, Day 3)

After lunch, the groups presented finished proposals to the managers for their response and approval. Whenever managers support the actions recommended in a proposal, I make sure that the community as a whole develops preliminary dates and milestones, and identifies people to perform the tasks associated with the proposal. (Usually at this point in the retrospective, there is enough commitment within the group that people are willing to volunteer for the tasks.)

The recommendations proposed by this group included the following.

- Reduce micro-management by having teams accept responsibility for assuring that their piece fits into the project architecture.
- Learn more about analyzing and designing systems and software before starting the coding phase of a project.
- Recognize that the group works in two modes: research and engineering. Learn to distinguish between the two modes, know when each is appropriate, and accept that

the engineering model is on par with, not inferior to, research.

This exercise was hard work, but once accomplished, it provided a vision for the group's future that would be better than the past. The community was now ready for one last exercise: the *"Making the Magic Happen" Exercise.* Holding this exercise at the end of the retrospective's three or four days is critical. A retrospective's ending can be magical. The community has worked hard; people are tired but feel comfortable discussing the project. Project members are now ready to talk about their most important issue, whatever it may be. All of the other discussions have been leading up to this moment.

Although each group's issue is unique, I've usually received clues about it throughout my interactions with the group—from my first discussions with the managers, from the pre-work I've assigned to members, from the one-on-one discussions, from casual conversations, and so on.

My guess was that this team's primary issue was that it had had *too much work.* Team members all had thought they were supposed to work long hours because everyone else did. The managers matched the engineers' hours because "they wanted to be with them." The engineers, in turn, saw their managers at work all the time and thought that any effort less than 140 percent was not good enough.

My strategy was clear to me: I needed to make it acceptable for people to discuss the topic, and then I would sit back and wait for the group to open up. To trigger the discussion for this particular group, I said, "Throughout this retrospective, I've been hearing about how much effort you gave to make this system a reality. I know that three members of your team were not able to be here because they were sick—probably because they were overworked. Take a few moments to reflect on what you personally sacrificed and note it on one of these index cards. These messages will remain private—I won't collect them. I just think it would be helpful for you to see your sacrifices written down."

After group members had listed their sacrifices on the cards, I invited people to share what they had written—if they chose to. I had seen enough risk-taking in this group to believe that my invitation would be sufficient to get things rolling.

The flood gates opened: One software developer talked about not being with his family on Sundays. Before the project, he reported, Sundays had been a special time. He stopped mid-sentence as his voice cracked and his eyes filled with tears. I encouraged him to stay with his feelings, and he continued to speak from his heart. Next, a manager talked about having been a cancer patient, and expressed his concern that the disease might recur because of the effort he had put into the project. Cautiously, others joined in, sharing what they had sacrificed. Throughout the session, support from the group was expressed for each person who spoke.

As the retrospective drew to a close, I got the team to agree on one thing: "Never again!" the group declared with feeling. I then suggested that each engineer, manager, and software developer place the index card in a special place as a reminder of this agreement. The suggestion was a good way to close the retrospective.

As a facilitator, was I prepared for the specific outcome? Yes, I was prepared, but not in the usual sense. A retrospective group goes where its members need to go. The facilitator's task is to help them get there, by

- watching the process and guiding it
- providing opportunities for all to be heard
- respecting everyone's opinions and privacy
- helping the group identify guidelines that yield healthy interactions
- being willing to work with emotions as they come up

Every group needs something different to make the magic happen. I have learned that my role as facilitator is to be fully present and to interact with the group, regardless of whatever concerns members raise. As a facilitator, I need to shed my personal preferences and be open to whatever discussion arises.

Some facilitators haven't learned to feel comfortable handling the emotional energy that can be generated during a retrospective, so they structure their retrospectives to avoid emotional situations. It has been my experience that when a retrospective is limited in this way, it is more difficult for the magic to happen, and the group may even feel that the retrospective has been a waste of time. It is worth the effort for a facilitator to learn how to work with emotions, so the team can have its magic moment and know that team members solved their most critical professional problem.

Preparing for the Facilitator's Job

At the end of the retrospective on which this sample is based, I looked back at my plan and confirmed that I had followed it fairly closely. I had dropped one exercise (the "Passive Analogy" Exercise) in order to provide two versions of the "Repair Damage Through Play" Exercise and I added the "Offer Appreciations" Exercise. To be truly effective, a facilitator must be ready to adjust the plan to fit what the group most needs, and then must help lead it to realization of that goal. A skilled facilitator has many tasks to accomplish. He or she must

- build trust within the community
- lead the exploration of difficult issues in a humane, caring, and effective manner
- ensure that managers participate, contribute, and learn, rather than dominate
- help the group to understand what its real issues are
- help team members find improved ways of working together

Because a retrospective facilitator in the software engineering field needs a broad range of skills, knowledge, and ability, it is advantageous if he or she is also a disciplined practitioner of software engineering and project management methods. Such a facilitator must know how to guide a group of people and how to manage conflict. He or she must be sensitive to emotion and know how to handle it, must be able to recognize team dynamics and how they affect the community, and must be ready to use all available tools and skills to help the community become more effective.

CHAPTER THREE

Engineering a Retrospective: Making Choices

After many years of toil, Ant decided it was time to get out of the old digs and buy a new place to live. He looked for an agent and found the perfect one at Busy Bee Realtors—Busy Bee himself. Not only was Bee's work ethic identical to Ant's, but Bee had experienced communal living and understood what his client wanted.

After assuring Ant that he would be able to find him the perfect home in no time, Bee flew off to start the search. Within minutes, Bee returned, full of details of a newly built condominium with a great view. He said that the current tenants were upscale and high-energy, just like Ant, and that the community association was very active, with every member working in harmony. Bee said it was so perfect, in fact, that were he not Ant's realtor, he would have bought it for himself.

Bee went on to explain that the condo was located several hundred yards away and told Ant that an offer should be made as soon as possible. Ant knew it could take him days to travel the distance, and trusting Bee's word, agreed to buy the condominium sight unseen. The papers were signed, the deed transferred, and Bee and Ant set a time to meet at the condominium.

Quite eager to see his new home, Ant set off on his journey at break-antenna speed. Realizing he had arrived well before the time that he and Bee had agreed to meet and unable to contain his excitement, Ant decided to tour the new condo on his own. As he approached his new home, however, Ant was shocked to discover that Bee had sold him space in a beehive—the condo was a waxy, six-sided affair without a single tunnel! After just a few minutes, Ant found that the neighbors' humming had gotten on his nerves, and that the temptation to sample the honey was overpowering, even though sampling was clearly against the association rules.

Bee arrived at the appointed time to find Ant irate and agitated. Even after learning what Ant objected to, Bee could not believe that the condo was not a perfect fit. In his mind, this condo had everything. . . .

[As this is a fable, fair reader, you may trust that insect attorneys got the mess straightened out eventually, but Bee was rather shaken by the whole experience. Here is what happened next.]

Bee went to Owl to see what he could learn. After intense discussion, Owl and Bee concluded that Bee had failed to understand a basic truth: One size does not fit all. The perfect fit for one type of client may be entirely wrong for another. Bee decided that he needed to better understand what his clients wanted, and to control his enthusiasm for what he himself considered desirable.

Watching Bee fly off, Owl congratulated himself, "Now, that retrospective went well. I think Bee learned something." He blinked rapidly for several seconds and then glanced downward as a rather forlorn and exhausted ant started to climb his tree.

The design principle of a beehive is that one size fits all. Once you have the perfect form, you need only replicate it and everyone will be happy. But Bee discovered that "one size does *not* fit all"—and this fact is true for retrospectives as well.

Bee's experience leads me to make two important observations about how to engineer retrospectives:

1) It is much easier to copy the format of a previous retrospective than to design one for a new situation, but *used* retrospective plans are not likely to fit well.
2) Each retrospective needs to be engineered to fit its unique environmental conditions and team dynamics.

In the most fundamental sense, we "engineer" retrospectives. *Webster's Ninth New Collegiate Dictionary* defines the verb "engineer" as *"to contrive or plan out usually with more or less subtle skill and craft,"* or, *"to guide the course of."* The following sections discuss this concept in greater detail.

ENGINEERING A RETROSPECTIVE

Although each retrospective needs to be uniquely tailored to the situation at hand, there are some common choices I have to make when I begin designing any new retrospective. In making these choices, I match my facilitator skills, experience, tools, and exercises to the particular environment and team dynamics. By environment and team dynamics, I mean the project, the people, the events that occurred during the project, the outcome, the attitudes, the objectives for the future, and so on. While the list of choices I need to make is the same, my decisions are always different, based on the various circumstances I need to take into account.

First Consideration: What is the purpose of this retrospective?

When I'm first contacted to help a team perform a retrospective, I always ask, "Why do you want it?" Usually, the question catches the prospective customer off guard. I get answers such as, "Because it was suggested during our last CMM audit."

"Because it is part of our corporate ISO 9000 process."
"Because we heard it was good to do." and "Hey, you're supposed to be the expert—don't you know?" Yes, actually, I do
know a number of reasons to perform a retrospective, and most
are better than those listed above.

At this point in the planning stage, I need to understand
what will be accomplished by holding this retrospective. I try
to find out for whom the learning is intended—management,
developers, or the whole team?

Each organization has different retrospective goals, and
until those are understood, I can't engineer a retrospective that
will meet the team's needs. Likewise, team members won't
know if the retrospective has been successful unless they know
what their goals were. A comment such as "You're the
expert—don't you know?" reveals something important—that
the organization doesn't know what it wants from a retrospective.

To uncover the real goals, I usually need to speak with a
number of people from the project. I often start by saying, "Tell
me about the project—just the really important stuff." After
hearing a number of responses, I begin to see what the organization wants to accomplish with the retrospective. I then
explore possible goals with the client.

Possible Goal # 1: Capture effort data. This goal quantifies the
actual effort expended on the project. The end of the project is
a perfect time to collect and record meaningful project data.

Possible Goal # 2: Get the story out. During any multi-person
project, a number of events occur that aren't known by the
whole group. In fact, on most projects, no one person knows
all the stories, and no one person knows how the pieces fit
together to tell the tale of the entire project. The whole story
needs to be told in a forum in which everyone can contribute.
It is the act of telling the story that eliminates the need for participants to waste time grumbling at the lunch table for months
to come. It is a way to put into context the situations that, by
themselves, may seem inconsequential, and a way to discover
heroic acts that went mostly unobserved. In short, telling the

story allows the whole group to understand exactly what happened and why.

Possible Goal # 3: Improve upon the process, procedures, management, and culture. By reflecting on what has occurred, we see things that we might do differently (and hopefully better) the next time around. And—just as important—we also discover what we did well and don't want to forget. When we reflect as a community rather than as individuals, the learning is greater. We see the whole, not just our individual piece.

Occasionally, this goal may get expressed as, "We need to fix Chris." Such a statement is usually accompanied by an explanation of what Chris did or didn't do and why the whole project failed because of Chris. Whenever I have looked more deeply into the "fix Chris" situation, I have discovered many issues for the whole team to work on improving, and Chris is only one part of the team's problem.

Possible Goal # 4: Capture collective wisdom. There are many firms that build teams for each project, rather than organize projects around an existing, long-term group. In this situation, the collective team wisdom acquired during the previous project is likely to be lost as individuals are scattered across the organization to support new undertakings. If, at the end of a project, the collective wisdom is discussed and documented, it becomes knowledge that survives the breakup of the team. People then are able to carry with them lessons learned by the team as well as those learned on their own.

Possible Goal # 5: Repair damage to the team. Creating and delivering a major piece of software is tough work. During the process, people are panicked and stressed, and they behave in uncharacteristic ways. Team members will be exhausted after putting out extreme amounts of energy and after making unreasonable personal sacrifices. Sometimes, things are said (or not said) in the heat of the moment. In each of these cases, relationships of all types will need mending.

All of this adds up to a problem that needs to be addressed. If team relationships have been damaged, a retrospective provides an excellent opportunity for colleagues to acknowledge hurt feelings and to evaluate the damage done in order to determine what must be repaired. A retrospective can provide a time to honor the heroic yet often unrecognized efforts of individuals. It should be seen as an opportunity to establish contacts that will help preserve relationships in the future. It is a time to engender honest enthusiasm for starting the next project.

Often, organizations reject this goal of repairing damage to the team because they take what I consider to be the archaic view that *it is not proper to deal with feelings in the workplace*. In my experience, high-performance teams are fully capable of developing safe ways to discuss the feelings and needs of each member.

Possible Goal # 6: Enjoy the accomplishment. As a rule, software developers are goal-oriented problem-solvers. They rarely stop to notice what they have accomplished. A retrospective provides an opportunity for such people to stop and reflect on how far they have come, rather than focus only on the current problem or the next one to be solved. Without such reflection, "post-project blues" can set in. If they have not taken time to savor the victory, people risk entering a new project without having recovered from the difficulties of the one just completed. The developer who suffers from "lost hope" feels that nothing will be better next time, and that the next project will be just as difficult and crazy.

Second Consideration: How healthy is this organization?

Another area to consider when designing a retrospective is how evolved the organizational culture is in the area of human interaction—that is, how do members of the team deal with difficult issues? Some cultures have developed highly functional ways of communicating with each other, working together, and solving problems, while others demonstrate dysfunctional behavior when faced with problems.

The table that follows shows a list of characteristics to look for when you identify a culture as either functional or dysfunctional.

Dysfunctional Cultures	Functional Cultures
• Guarded language and secrets.	• Honest communication.
• Distrust of other groups.	• Alliance and cooperation with other groups.
• Well-defined boundaries between groups; lots of discussion over who has a particular responsibility; management-driven.	• Boundaries are mutually discussed and agreed upon between groups; participant-driven.
• Blame and lack of respect for other groups.	• Appreciation and effective use of differences between various groups.
• Skepticism of someone else's new idea or approach. Rewards for fighting someone else's idea.	• Group refinement of an individual's idea. Careful evaluation once experimentation with the idea has been performed.
• Pressure to produce.	• Encouragement to improve.
• Behavior, process, and activities highly influenced by past.	• Situations handled in the present with creative new solutions.
• Strong pressure to conform to the standard.	• Flexibility available for situations that are unique or new.
• Individual competition and survival are key issues. Looking good is the way to progress.	• High-quality results are the key issues for the team as a whole. Helping everyone look good is the way to progress.
• Meetings are combative.	• Meetings are constructive.
• Developers and managers feel powerless to change the organization.	• Developers and managers take action to improve their organization.

42

Dysfunctional Cultures	Functional Cultures
• Decision-making involves having things your way. Often the discussion centers around "the best way" to accomplish something.	• Decision-making is consensus-driven.
• During decision-making, proof of concept is required from colleagues; distrust of ideas and approaches is the foundation of the working relationship.	• During decision-making, respect for and trust of colleagues' skills is obvious.

Your own observation regarding the degree of involvement of a culture is very important. The less functional an organization, the more effort you will need to put into ensuring that the retrospective stays focused in a healthy direction—on learning rather than on fault-finding.

It's important to note that no organization is likely to be totally functional or totally dysfunctional. There is a continuum along which most organizations lie, falling somewhere between the two extremes. The table can be used as a starting point for an understanding of the approximate state of the culture, and perhaps to begin a dialogue with the client about areas for improvement.

The greater the dysfunction, the fewer retrospective design choices you have. With highly dysfunctional organizations, either you need to be skilled at dealing with personal interactions and antagonism or you need to lower the goals of the retrospective to avoid serious conflict.

I do not recommend avoiding difficult issues, since limiting the scope of a retrospective brings little benefit to the client. Instead, I focus portions of the retrospective on ways to improve the health of the organization.

Third Consideration: Do I have the skills to lead this retrospective?

Whatever the health of an organization, two other factors that must be considered in the design of a retrospective are, first, your own skills as a facilitator and, second, your level of understanding about the work done during the project. The fact is, a given facilitator may not be sufficiently qualified and/or ready to lead certain retrospectives. Below are some criteria to use when evaluating your own or another's ability to lead a particular retrospective.

A facilitator must be an outsider. A facilitator needs to be an outsider rather than a member of the project team. Facilitators need to remain neutral during the retrospective—watching the process, building a safe environment, helping people participate, summarizing points as the story lines begin to weave, and encouraging the exploration of alternatives. *A facilitator must be technically competent.* A good retrospective facilitator needs to have software development experience in order to understand the nature of the work done during the project. The more a facilitator knows about what is to be reviewed, the better he or she will be at leading discussions and helping the team move toward a collective understanding. As facilitator, you should understand the project's process, architecture, tools, components, companion groups, suppliers, vocabulary, and so on.

A facilitator must be a Betazoid. Because a retrospective involves leading people through a number of exercises (some designed to cause individuals to think, others designed to encourage group discussion), a facilitator must be able to manage both people who talk too much and people who don't talk enough. The facilitator must establish and maintain an environment in which it is safe to speak out about unpleasant, embarrassing, or emotional issues. The facilitator needs to be skilled at resolving conflict, mediating, and helping transform blame into constructive information. He or she must be able to sense the emotion of the team as the retrospective proceeds. In short, a facilitator needs the skills of Deanna Troy, the telepathic Betazoid counselor from *Star Trek: The Next Generation.* Luckily, these skills can be learned—see Chapter 9 for details and refer to my Website: *http://www.retrospectives.com.*

All that having been said, you *can* lead a retrospective even if you don't presently have all the required knowledge and skills. It is possible to form a facilitation *team* by employing one person who is skilled in software development and a second person who is skilled in managing personal interactions.

A True Story

After I had led a very successful retrospective, one of the participating managers invited me to work with his team on its next project. During this effort, I introduced analysis modeling techniques, object-oriented design, quality assurance techniques, project-management improvement methods, and several other skills to change the culture of the group.

In the middle of the project, the manager left the team and I was asked to serve as acting manager. Eventually, a replacement was hired—a manager who focused more on budget than on process improvement—and I resumed my role as a member of the team.

When the project ended, I scheduled a retrospective, but explained to the new manager that I could not facilitate since I was part of the team. I recommended a colleague to run the retrospective, but the manager responded that he could not justify the cost of paying me to attend the retrospective as a contributor while also paying someone else to serve as facilitator. Because he'd heard I was an experienced facilitator, he believed I could play both roles.

While my ego tempted me to give it a try, my wisdom won out. I'd witnessed too many failures by people who had attempted to both facilitate and participate in a retrospective. In such a dual role, my focus would have been divided. When I spoke, there would be confusion as to whether I was speaking as facilitator or as participant. To do both would be unfair to the group and to me. Since it didn't seem as though the manager would change his mind, I had two choices: Cancel the retrospective, or hire the facilitator I had recommended we use and then pay for her services myself.

The first option seemed completely wrong. We had created a team that viewed holding a retrospective as essential to any professional software group's growth. Canceling the retrospective would have been equivalent to saying, "Our team doesn't need to continue to grow." An additional reason for my commitment to holding the retrospective was that, during the project, I had encouraged team members to contribute suggestions on process improvement, but because of scheduling difficulties, I had asked them to save some of their new ideas for the retrospective. I felt my credibility was on the line.

The second option seemed extreme. The idea that I should have to pay for my client to learn about process improvement struck me as intolerable, but the truth was, such a great team deserved a good retrospective experience (and a better manager!)—and so I selected the second option. I paid for the facilitator, justifying the expense as a gift to team members with whom I had truly enjoyed working. At the same time, I decided that I needed to find a new client.

Armed with knowledge about the three areas of consideration (goals, organizational health, and your own skills as facilitator), you now can finalize details about your retrospective design. The questions in the following sections should help you plan.

WHO SHOULD ATTEND THE RETROSPECTIVE?

In my early retrospectives, I included software developers only. In particular, managers were excluded. My rationale was that software developers would be more likely to discuss problems about management if their managers were not in the room.

My main goal in these early retrospectives was to develop a report for managers that recommended various changes. We would work very hard on the report, then deliver it to management, hold briefings, and try in various ways to communicate to the managers what we had learned about the project. The long-term results were usually disappointing, and very little would change within the organization. I now believe that one reason the results of those early retrospectives were poor was because the managers had not participated in the retrospective, so they were not privy to the discussions that led to the recommendations, and therefore did little to see that the recommendations become practice.

INCLUDE ENTIRE CAST OF CHARACTERS

Managers do need to be involved in retrospectives. Furthermore, since we are looking at the whole project, we need to include key people from external organizations involved in the development effort. Over time, my retrospectives have shifted from small, intimate gatherings to larger, somewhat-more-inclusive sessions.

Based on my experience, I have developed a list of retrospective candidates, categories of personnel who may know something informative about the project. Not everyone on the list gets invited, but as I work through the categories of candidates, my clients often think of additional people. The list includes people from the following areas:

- marketing
- sales
- technical support
- customer support
- customer training
- quality assurance
- procurement

- manufacturing
- key customers
- hardware and software developers
- technical writers
- third-party vendors
- contractors

One important but often overlooked person to include is someone who may have a truly unique view of the project: the department secretary.

I try to involve as many viewpoints as possible in a retrospective while keeping the group small enough to be managed. Usually, my clients can identify individuals with an important piece of the story to tell as we work through the list together.

How many people participate in a retrospective affects how it should be designed, its length and cost, as well as what level of demands are made on the facilitator. The largest group for which I have served as sole facilitator consisted of nearly thirty people. That particular team scored quite high on the functional chart, and the project was perceived as a success. For larger groups, or ones in which the culture is less evolved or the project has elements of failure, I generally build a team of facilitators. The largest team of facilitators I've worked with consisted of four people. We led a cross-departmental retrospective of a failed project, with a total of 68 participants.

WHERE SHOULD THE RETROSPECTIVE BE HELD?

A retrospective can be held *on site*, *off-site local*, or *off-site residential*. An *on-site* location has the advantage of being less expensive for the company than a *residential* session. Other advantages include the probability that the site is familiar to and easily accessed by the participants, that other project members who are not part of the retrospective can be consulted when needed, and that project artifacts not gathered before the start of the retrospective are readily available. But an *on-site* meeting has disadvantages: It may be seen by participants as cheap and therefore not important, the site is "the same old place," the retrospective is easily interrupted, and participants may not prepare as well since they can duck out to look for whatever materials they need at the last minute.

In cases in which the project's budget has been depleted or holding an off-site meeting is against the organization's policy, I have facilitated on-site retrospectives, but I usually have found that the team achieved far less than it would have accomplished if the retrospective had been held off-site. Even when a retrospective is held at a premium on-site location (such as the executive dining room or the corporate boardroom) and a "do not disturb" policy is established, the participants seem to offer the "same old thinking" and the "same old behavior" that crippled the project itself. Limitations seem easier to accept and new ideas easier to kill when a retrospective is held on-site. In short, the on-site retrospective isn't seen as having any long-term significance. Because of this, I no longer facilitate on-site retrospectives.

When deciding between recommending an *off-site local* or an *off-site residential* retrospective, I consider the needs of the group in the context of the available budget. A residential retrospective is the most costly, of course, but it provides the best opportunity for participants to learn how to change the way future work will be performed. Around-the-clock immersion yields amazing understanding, learning, and growth. For most participants, a residential off-site meeting will be seen as a form of reward or benefit. The feeling of gratitude this evokes makes the retrospective an important part of the project, and residential retrospective participants tend to work harder and learn more than participants in other types of retrospectives.

A local, off-site location from which participants return home at night has the advantage of being considerably less expensive than a residential, but the depth of learning is less and the potential for real improvement is smaller.

The decision to hold a residential meeting is usually made by someone very high up in management or by an upper-level manager rather than by the project manager. Neither of these higher-level managers is likely to be close to the project and may not understand the potential value of a residential retrospective. Typically, the high-level manager must veto all sorts of proposals and may automatically reject the residential retrospective option without giving it much thought, perhaps because it sounds like a boondoggle or because the money simply isn't available for a residential meeting.

If the money really is not there, then an off-site, local retrospective becomes a reasonable choice, but I do not settle for one until I have urged the decision-maker to calculate the cost of a residential retrospective compared with a non-residential one, including participants' salaries and the cost of lost days of work, to see exactly how much money is involved. The incremental cost of a residential meeting over the cost of a non-residential is often quite small.

In a case in which the decision-maker is worried that the off-site facility is some sort of a boondoggle, I describe what I usually see at a residential retrospective—people working very hard, often well into the night. With the project manager, I discuss ways to reassure the decision-maker about the value of the retrospective, and look for goals common to both the project manager and the decision-maker. For example, I might propose we lower costs by choosing a truly no-frills location, such as a scout camp during the off-season, or that we lower the boondoggle component by choosing a site with no discernible fun quotient (certainly not a site near a golf course!). Actually, this no-frills, sensible location is the type of site I prefer, for reasons discussed more fully in the next section.

Selecting a Residential Site

For any retrospective, I need a room large enough to hold the entire team, plus several break-out spaces for smaller groups—ideally one area per four or five people. With schedule slips likely, reserving a residential location before the end of a project is difficult. As a result, residentials usually end up at rustic places that are not in high demand, and that require a bit of travel. These limitations actually turn out to be benefits.

If the space selected for the residential retrospective is too rustic, that is, if it is run-down or bare-bones, the participants usually work together to make it more comfortable. If it takes at least two hours to drive to the site and there is limited parking, all the better—I want team members to carpool. Driving together enables people to talk, to re-establish relationships, and to discuss the past project, the next project, and the retrospective. And, since people coming and going disturbs the process, holding the meeting some distance away limits the temptation for people to return to work to attend to "important" business or to their homes for personal reasons.

WHEN SHOULD THE RETROSPECTIVE BE HELD?

The best time to hold the retrospective is from one to three weeks after the end of the project. It makes no sense to have a retrospective before the project is completed, and even less to hold it after the next project has begun. Scheduling is tricky, since the schedule needs to be projected before the project ends, resulting in a great deal of guessing about the actual dates.

As a seasoned facilitator, I know dates slip. My business is service-oriented, and so I work hard to keep my schedule open enough to accommodate these slips. I also keep close tabs on a project as it nears its end so that I can use my finely honed sense of intuition to estimate when the project is likely to finish.

I never hold a retrospective immediately after the end of a project; at that point, no one has the necessary energy. Team members need a break—some time to sleep, to re-connect with family and friends, to take care of postponed personal business, and to do a bit of reorganizing at work.

How Long Should a Retrospective Be?

Simply stated, effective retrospectives require about three days.

I once received e-mail from a person whose manager had allocated one hour for a retrospective of a six-month project. The writer of the e-mail had been assigned the responsibility for making sure the retrospective would be a success, and she was looking for advice. My response to her was that so brief a retrospective could not be successful.

While I have heard of retrospectives being held in an hour, or in half a day, the following comments sum up those brief attempts:

We tried retrospectives. After a while, we discovered that each review was making the same recommendations. Clearly, nothing was changing, so we decided that retrospectives are a waste of time. We don't do them anymore.

It is sad to know that such an effective learning tool as a retrospective was ruined in part because not enough time was allocated to do one properly. I find it ironic that "waste of time" was cited as the group's reason to avoid retrospectives, when the problem was that the group had not allowed *enough* time in the first place!

It is unreasonable to believe that significant learning about a multi-person project that lasted several months can occur in an hour. At best, such a brief retrospective may serve to identify a few symptoms of real problems, but participants are unlikely to be able to do more than recommend poorly analyzed, partial solutions that do not fully address the issues.

There are two probable arguments the decision-maker will make for keeping the retrospective brief: First, he or she may cite insufficient funds to pay for the longer retrospective. Second, he or she may believe that a longer retrospective cannot produce results commensurate with the time it will take. The project manager may also argue against holding a full retrospective because of a secret wish to avoid the detailed scrutiny involved with a longer review of the project while still appearing to favor holding one.

The first reason, lack of money, can be repudiated with some numbers. For example, during a six-month project, just one member of a team is likely to work a minimum of 120 days on up to 150 days (or more if that person works weekends in addition to evenings). A three-day review takes less than 3 percent of the project time—a very small portion of the budget—and a well-run retrospective can be expected to cut six days or more off the next project, yielding a 100 percent return on investment.

We can counter the second argument by providing information about what happens at a retrospective, sharing stories about successful retrospectives, and by describing the results retrospectives bring to an organization.

If the resistance derives from a person's wish to avoid a serious review, the facilitator would do better to refuse to hold the retrospective at all than to risk using it inappropriately or where it is not wanted. However, before I refuse to participate, I try to change the decision-maker's or project manager's attitude. Generally, I begin by questioning the person to try to understand the nature of his or her reluctance. Once I have an individual's fears in perspective, I see whether I can be reassuring that my approach will facilitate a safe retrospective. Often, a person's fear is based on a single bad experience, so I try to learn what happened in the past, and then explain what will be different this time.

> A word of advice: Don't be afraid to say no to an invitation to lead a retrospective if you think the participants (and especially the management team) are not committed to learning how to do things better. Be particularly wary if you think the true motivation for holding the retrospective is management's desire to find scapegoats.

A True Story

I was contacted by Eric, an administrative assistant to a high-level manager whom we'll call Ron. Ron wanted Eric to schedule a retrospective to be held in about six weeks. After our initial discussion, I told Eric I thought a retrospective would be a good idea, and asked him to set up a meeting with Ron so we could discuss the details of the retrospective.

For five weeks, Eric and I scheduled and re-scheduled meetings, but Ron always needed to be somewhere else at the last minute. He was at emergency meetings related to getting the software project finished, away on an emergency trip visiting customers, on an emergency vacation with his family, and so on.

Finally, with the retrospective scheduled to begin in just one week, I still had not had a chance to discuss goals and choices with Ron, and so I suggested to Eric that we postpone the retrospective indefinitely until everyone had had a chance to slow down, think, and plan.

Eric told Ron my recommendation. Ron's response as he ran out the door was predictable: "Definitely not! We need to learn how to prevent all these emergencies. Tell Norm that I don't have time to meet with him. Maybe he should just plan on winging it, and we can talk during the retrospective."

When Eric reported this conversation to me, I knew why Ron had so many emergencies: He didn't take time to plan. It would not have surprised me if this became Ron's major realization as a result of the retrospective. Yet I knew we wouldn't get to that point—I couldn't proceed with the retrospective because I knew that to do so would only invite more emergencies.

I gave Eric the following brief message to convey to Ron: "I can't lead a retrospective until you have time to sit down and plan it with me. As a result, I'm canceling my plans to lead the retrospective next week. Please call me when you have the time to plan."

Ron never called. He was too busy, right up to the day he was fired.

CHAPTER FOUR

Selling a Retrospective

"Who? Who?" Owl asked as he peered down from his porch. "Oh, it's you, Beaver. Where are you going?"

Beaver stopped short and looked up into the tree to answer Owl. "It's not where I'm going, it's where I've been. I was visiting the Alligator Alliance. I tried to sell them on the idea of building a new swamp."

Curious to know more, Owl asked, "How did your meeting go?"

"I tried to use my best engineering logic," replied Beaver. "I showed the alligators exactly where the humans have changed the water flow just upstream from their swamp. I included water-flow measurements, calculations, hydro-dynamic projections, and photographs showing how the humans breached my dams. It's obvious to the casual observer that the swamp will get smaller every year for the next three until there will be no swamp left. I explained how, in my years of experience with humans, I've found that they don't give up on these projects." Beaver took a deep breath before continuing. "The only logical response is to build a new swamp over in Never-Build-Here Valley."

Owl probed, "Did they buy into your proposal?"

Showing obvious disappointment," Beaver replied, "No, they didn't. But their refusal doesn't make sense. There is no logical reason not to build a new swamp. Alligators are just stupid!"

Owl was considering how best to give Beaver some suggestions on selling his idea to the alligators when Beaver changed the subject. "By the way, Owl, I passed the levee that directs water around your tree. It should be built out another foot or two longer, given the new water-flow projections. Do you want me to work on it?"

"Sure," replied Owl, as he watched Beaver scurry away.

Beaver is an engineer. He doesn't know how to sell and, like many technical professionals, he doesn't want to know. Nevertheless, for retrospectives to flourish, facilitators need to learn how to sell, if only just a little.

I have a special place in my heart for people who set out to sell an organization on trying its first retrospective. Whether you are a retrospective facilitator, a member of a community that is ending a project, or an advocate in a software engineering process group—you are on a bold and noble path. In an ideal world, you would use Beaver's approach. You would attempt to sell management simply by describing the process and activities of a retrospective and conclude by saying, "This is a good thing and it is obviously cost-effective. Decide now to do it."

However, as Beaver discovered, this is not an ideal world and this approach never works unless management has already been sold, which means that the selling was done earlier by someone else. Let's look more closely at how to sell the idea of a retrospective.

UNDERSTANDING THE MARKET FOR RETROSPECTIVE SALES

Begin by analyzing the retrospective-buying marketplace. You can divide it into three segments: First are those potential clients who want to change their software development process because change is a habit. Second are those who want to change because of the pain or crisis experienced during the project. Third are those who don't want to change their process at all because they think the status quo is good enough.

Each of these segments has its own special needs and is motivated by unique factors, so your approach to selling retrospectives must vary according to your customer. The figure shown on the following page illustrates market opportunity and ease of sale.

By looking at the figure, we can see that a community in Segment 1, in which continuous process improvement is a habit, will readily accept the idea of a retrospective. The team has learned to look at its development process and improve it every day—in fact, improving its process is regarded as a crucial part of the job, and the team's track record shows it. If team members have not yet participated in a retrospective, the most likely reason is that they either don't know about the technique, haven't found a good facilitator, or have tried it but did not have a good format for facilitation. It strikes me as a sad fact that there are too few teams in the software engineering field that consistently and reliably produce excellent software at reduced cost in the expected time frame.

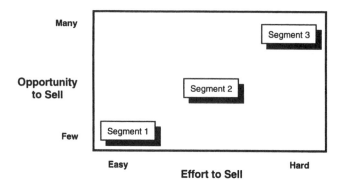

At the other end of the spectrum are numerous groups that fall into Segment 3. These groups rarely consider the idea of seeking ways to improve their process. In such groups, attention to process is lost in the urgency to solve the immediate problems of creating software. At first glance, you will see little motivation for such groups to consider a retrospective. It doesn't mean you shouldn't try to sell to this segment; it just means that the sell will require more effort and more time. Even after all that, there is little likelihood that the Segment 3 group will buy into holding a retrospective. You will need to find a "mass market" approach, relying on numbers to find the few groups interested in trying a retrospective. These few groups may be making their first effort toward moving to Segment 1, or sadly, have recently and painfully moved into Segment 2.

Segment 2 contains groups that have experienced difficulties during their previous project. Their project struggled to the end. Schedules slipped, technology let them down, customers were unhappy, or possibly the project was stopped before the software was produced. While change is not a habit for such a group, its members are now aware that something different needs to be done. The problem, however, is that they aren't certain what that is. A retrospective will be foreign to them. The idea that individuals within their community have something valuable to learn from each other, that they can discover ways to improve their work process, or that this learning can be done in a positive manner will be suspect. Nevertheless, a team that is in this segment is a good prospect.

Segment 1 Sales Approach (Change As Habit)

To sell a retrospective to managers in a Segment 1 environment, ask them how they have gone about identifying aspects in their software process that they want to improve. Ask them to describe all aspects of change they find intimidating. Explain the retrospective process, demonstrate that you are competent, and tell them ways a retrospective can complement their current approach to improving software process. You might share with them details from Chapter 2, "Anatomy of a Retrospective," or even better, write a version based on your own experience leading retrospectives but tailored to fit the current situation.

Segment 2 Sales Approach (Change Due to Pain)

To sell Segment 2 customers, begin by assuring management that the community can find ways to prevent a similar painful experience from occurring on future projects. Help the managers see that if the community does not learn, the likelihood of a recurrence of the experience is great. Help them understand that software development practice can improve. Explain Kerth's Prime Directive for retrospectives and discuss ways to make a retrospective a positive learning experience. Ask the managers what concerns they have about the retrospective and respond with facts from a few of your own True Stories.

Segment 3 Sales Approach (No Change Requested)

Plan on waging a long sales campaign and use frequency of the message as your main sales tool. Your goal will be to accomplish one or more of the following:

- Help the team shift into Segment 1 or 2, and then proceed with the sales approach for that segment.
- If team members have shifted by themselves, help them realize they have moved into Segment 1 (or 2), and then work with them to set up a retrospective.
- Build a relationship and wait for team members to realize they need to set moving into Segment 1 as a goal.

When I use the expression "frequency of the message," I mean that you should use a combination of mailings, phone calls, and lunches to accomplish this ongoing dialogue and to build your relationship with the Segment 3 customer. Position yourself not just as a retrospectives expert, but also as a clearinghouse of software engineering information—an expert in the whole field and, as such, the first one they think to call whenever they have a question.

Periodically, touch base with managers in the community and discuss whatever difficulties they are having. Do what you can to keep communication channels open. From time to time, share stories with them about how a particular retrospective benefited another similar community. Use the lessons learned from other retrospectives not to push the idea of retrospectives themselves, but to share the wisdom. Take every opportunity to educate the managers about how a retrospective can help their teams improve their software process. Let them know that if they ever need help, you are available.

SELLING IS OKAY

I used to feel morally and physically uncomfortable—even sleazy—when I would try to sell people something. It seemed that, by selling to them, I was intruding on their right of privacy, their own pursuit of happiness, and their right to decide for themselves. I hated it when salespeople telephoned me, and I didn't want to be involved with that aspect of doing business. It wasn't until one day when I went to buy a used car that my way of thinking changed, as the following true story illustrates.

A True Story

For years I dreamed of owning a Mercedes-Benz 450 SL, a luxury sports car. I knew I'd probably never be able to afford a brand-new car, but I had convinced myself that the 450 SL would run great for 300,000 miles, and that a used Mercedes would be a sound purchase. I headed to the nearest Mercedes dealership, looking for a well-used car, and was greeted by Rick, the salesman on duty when I arrived.

I told Rick exactly what I was looking for, but instead of showing me the 450 SL's he had for sale, he invited me into his office to talk more about what I wanted in my dream car. I admitted that I wanted the status of driving a luxury sports car, but that I also wanted the safety for which Mercedes-Benz is well known. I described how I needed a car that could carry my drums, and that I also needed dependability. I told Rick I wanted the performance of the sports car, but conceded that I most likely would never put the top down.

Armed with this information about my driving needs, Rick proceeded to convince me that I was looking for the wrong car. With great mastery, he helped me discover that I really wanted to buy a used Mercedes 190 sedan. I learned from him that the 190 had newer safety technology than the 450 SL, and that the 190 would be able to carry my drums, would be reliable, and had a performance option that would satisfy my dreams—oh, and by the way, it was a good bit cheaper.

I left the car lot impressed with the notion that Rick was not trying to "sell" me, but rather that he was interested in helping me make *the right decision for me.* Signing the sales papers on the 190 several days later, I mentioned to Rick and his manager how much I appreciated that, instead of selling me "a car," Rick decided to help me find the car that was perfect for me.

They both smiled and Rick quietly replied, "The business of selling, at its best, is nothing more than helping the customer make the right choice." Suddenly I realized that selling, when the customer's best interest is the prime focus, can be a virtuous activity.

If you truly believe that a retrospective event is in a group's best interest, why not say it? Why not say it several ways, and say it over time? Why not think of ways you can help your customer make a decision that he or she will deeply appreciate for years to come? Don't be afraid of helping a customer make the right decision—"selling" to him or her is not done for your own gain, but for the customer's greater good. If you don't believe a retrospective is right for a customer, then don't sell it; but if it is right, then you do a disservice by not speaking up.

"Qualify" the Customer

When talking with a person who expresses interest in holding a retrospective, you need to "qualify" that person early in the discussion. Is he or she the person who will decide whether to hold the retrospective? If you can determine that you are talking with a qualified buyer, keep going. If not, you are talking to someone who perhaps would *like* to have a retrospective, but who, at best, will be your contact person. Ask this contact person to help you understand who the qualified buyer is and have him or her arrange a meeting between you and the decision-maker. Bring the contact person along if doing so makes sense, but realize that no sale will occur until you talk to the decision-maker.

EFFECTIVE SELLING REQUIRES LISTENING

As I learned from my experience with the car salesman, you must learn what's important to the decision-maker before you try to sell a retrospective. Ask about goals for the group, difficulties running projects, and changes made. Find out how well the changes work. Ask about the decision-maker's hopes and fears, and get to know what's important to him or her. Once you know all this, you are in an excellent position to help the decision-maker identify whether to hold a retrospective.

Sell Trust, Confidence, and Ongoing Support

The retrospective event is your product, but it is only a piece of what you are selling. You are also selling yourself as the best facilitator for the job. Demonstrate your facilitation and listening skills, as well as your understanding of the team's project experience. Build your contact's trust in you by being honest and confident about your abilities. Discuss the scope of your follow-up support to help implement the changes identified during the retrospective. You are not there just for the duration of the retrospective—you will also be there to help establish lasting change.

CHAPTER FIVE

Preparing for a Retrospective

Owl noticed Singed-Tail, the wolf formerly known as Big Bad Wolf, reading a cookbook entitled Swine in Wine. *"Are you thinking about making another run at those pigs?" Owl asked, as he gently landed on a branch above him.*

Singed-Tail growled, "Yep, and this'll get me prepared."

Owl probed, "Have you read anything else?"

"Nope," Wolf responded.

"Nothing at all?" Owl asked disbelievingly.

"No, not recently. . . . What are ya gettin' at, Owl?"

"Well, I've seen some of the other wolves reading The Sage Wolf's Complete Guide to Hunting. *I was just wondering if you might want to paw through the Getting Prepared section for a few good ideas. Maybe it will alert you to something you've missed."*

Singed-Tail yawned. "I read that book—a long time ago. It was just a bunch of common sense. Nothin' to howl about. I'd rather be chewin' on a weasel bone than readin' that stuff again. Now scram before I get hungry and reconsider my no-chicken policy!"

Having been rudely made aware of Singed-Tail's disinterest in his advice, Owl quietly flew off. Upon reflection, Owl realized that Singed-Tail didn't understand why the wolf elders wrote their guide—to share their wisdom and to list all the things they had overlooked when they were young and inexperienced.

But did he have to call him chicken?

Human nature (and, as the fable shows, wolf nature, too!) makes it hard for people to appreciate the value of certain kinds of information unless it can be used immediately. Back when Singed-Tail had read the Getting Prepared section in the hunting guidebook, he wasn't getting ready for a hunt. So, at the time, his reaction was that the advice contained nothing useful to him.

I suspect that this chapter on preparation may be best appreciated when you are actively preparing to lead a retrospective. The information may seem like common sense to the first-time reader, but the message I want to convey is that preparing fully for a retrospective is essential to your success.

If this is your first reading of this book, you may want to skim this chapter, looking at the cartoons and reading the True Story section before moving on. This approach is fine, so long as you come back to study the contents when you prepare for a retrospective. For now, I ask you to remember how foolish Singed-Tail was to conclude that information on preparation isn't worth studying! For those wanting specifics, this chapter provides key information on how a facilitator can get ready for a retrospective, including how to prepare the participants (both developers and managers) and how to secure their involvement.

CONNECT WITH THE MANAGERS

The first job in getting prepared involves learning ways to connect with management. Even though retrospectives are a powerful way for managers to improve control of projects—that is, to change what didn't work into a strategy for future success— not all managers like the idea. Not all see retrospectives as *a way to learn how to manage better*. Some managers fear that the retrospective will become a public review of their ability to manage. Others believe that they already know what needs to be changed, and only want to use the retrospective as a way to get their staff members to buy into the obvious. Still other managers see a retrospective as a waste of time, but think that it is politically advantageous to put on a show of having one. Even those managers who do support the retrospective and see it as an opportunity for improvement may find it difficult to give up being a leader to become a listener during the retrospective process. For these reasons, facilitators must start by establishing a sound working relationship with project management. The steps I use to connect with management follow.

The first activity I undertake is to meet with the managers to give them information about myself, to get a sense of why a retrospective is important to them, to discover what they hope will happen, and to learn what they fear. I believe a face-to-face meeting works best, but I have also used telephone conference calls, followed by conversations with specific individuals.

At the beginning of the meeting or conference call, I introduce myself, describing whatever personal credentials I feel are appropriate to the specific situation. I then go on to define the goals of a retrospective, to briefly describe some of my experiences with retrospectives I believe to be relevant, and finally to summarize the results that can be achieved. My objectives in this part of the introductory session are to

- give the managers a chance to develop a sense of who I am and of how I work
- present a general idea of what will happen at the retrospective
- convey the idea that a retrospective is a learning process rather than a fault-finding experience
- establish a vision of the possibilities

By means of this session, I hope to eliminate any lingering fear, to increase the managers' understanding of how a retrospective can help with the particular project's problems, and to secure support. In particular, I need the managers' help in presenting the idea of a retrospective to their people and I want them to be able to answer questions that get asked most frequently.

Then, I change the focus. Because I want to know exactly what the managers think about holding a retrospective, I ask questions such as

- What would you like to accomplish by having a retrospective?
- What would a successful retrospective look like to you?
- What would you like to have happen after the retrospective?
- Why are you asking me to lead this retrospective?
- What are your greatest fears about this retrospective?
- What topics need to be addressed?
- What topics do I need to be careful with—and why?

- What details about people can you share that I should know?

Usually, my final question is, "What questions do you have for me—about my background, the retrospective process, or anything else?"

After I have answered any questions asked of me, I describe how I think the retrospective might proceed, and I invite the managers to suggest ideas as well. I explain that, as a team, we will work together to develop the retrospective goals. I call goals from the first session "initial goals" since they are likely to change as we work through the retrospective. Typical initial goals are listed below.

- Explore why we had such difficulty in making a schedule we could trust.
- Discuss how to discover if a programmer is blocked and how to react without committing the sin of micromanagement.
- Determine whether we spent the right amount of time in the analysis phase.
- Discuss how we might reorganize the team for the next project.
- Learn how to do a better job at interviewing, managing, and overseeing contract help.
- Decide whether we should put more effort into patterns and components for the next project or if we should scrap the idea.
- Find ways to help Bob in Testing get his job done.

This list provides a good starting point, and as we deviate from these initial goals, we use the list as a management tool—scratching out, adding, and changing goals as required.

One practice we must agree upon is that managers will not participate heavily in the retrospective discussion. Their main responsibility is to listen and learn. A second responsibility of the management team is to provide insight from their perspective to address issues raised by software developers and other participants. Before the retrospective, I work out a system of signals with the managers that I can use during the event. For example, I will use one signal to say to the manager, "You are participating too much right now—try just listening for a while." A manager will have another signal to tell me, "I really need to comment right now!"

Often, it is hard for managers to stop leading and to play the role of observer. I know from personal experience that when I have been the designated leader on a project, I have found it very difficult to shift my role to that of participant during the retrospective. In those situations, I usually need to be reminded about consciously suspending my leadership role. For managers who are really having a hard time just listening, I suggest that they take detailed notes that can serve as triggers for later discussion. I tell them I will meet with them at break time to look over the notes to see if we need to do any redirecting of the process. I also tell managers that they can hold "staff meetings" at meal breaks if, during the retrospective, they need to discuss any issues about work on current projects.

Map the Community

As a way to further understand the project's dimensions, I have the managers help me develop a "map"—that is, a version of an organizational chart—identifying the community that worked on the project. The map helps me understand working relationships between project team members, and the act of creating it provides an informal setting in which the managers can tell me their view of what went right and what went wrong.

To create the map, I need to know the following:

- What was the formal reporting structure? Did it change over time? If so, how? Who filled each position, and what were their responsibilities? When did they start in this role and when did they stop?
- What were the important informal relationships that existed during the project? How strong were those relationships? Did they aid or hinder project progress?

As the map is developed, and as personnel and roles are discussed, you may hear unfamiliar acronyms or abbreviations, such as CHE, GMAS, BIM, and so forth. This is the perfect time to write down what these letter combinations mean. My preference is to include them as a legend on the map. Instead of using a standard notation, I usually make something up that best fits the individual situation. However, there are a few conventions I use frequently—both for formal and informal reporting relationships:

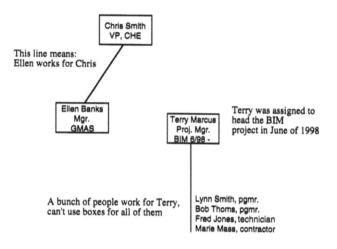

For informal or special relationships, I use a different type of line:

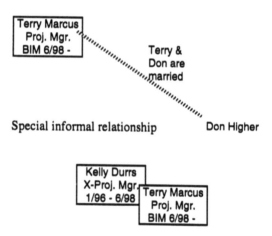

Sometimes, I make up the notation as I hear the story. For example, a line with many bars dissecting it shows a relationship with problems.

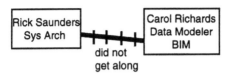

A piece of the story to come

Below is an example of a representative organizational map:

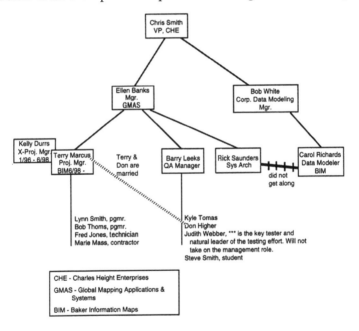

A real company's organizational chart would differ from my example in at least two ways: First, there would be more informal relationships; and second, the diagram would not be as neat! Usually, a chart depicting a real project's organization becomes messy rather quickly, since the relationships exist in a way that defies a clean drawing. Also, reorganizations are common, and capturing both the "before" and "after" of an organization can be a real challenge.

There are many reasons why I recommend doing an organizational map, but prime among them are the following:

- The map helps the facilitator understand relationships among people in the organization.
- Drawing the map prompts the managers to begin to tell the story from their perspective (such as, how people were deployed).
- The activity is an introduction to a bit of project history—when people joined, left, were reassigned, and so forth.
- The map helps identify who should attend the retrospective.
- Legend annotations help clarify the abbreviations and acronyms used on this particular project.

COLLECT EFFORT DATA

Slipped schedules and cost overruns are all too common on software projects. Given this fact, I'm surprised at how few people actively measure and record the money and time expended on a project. I often ask clients how much they spend to produce a line of code. They rarely know. It seems to me that anyone who is serious about improving cost and schedule estimates needs accurate data from past projects.

In cases in which the client doesn't know the cost, I incorporate the task of capturing effort data into the retrospective process as a benefit to the client, but effort data also is useful to me. As the retrospective leader, I know that solid numbers on effort and cost help me understand the size and difficulty of the project. As I work with my clients to collect the data, I look for answers to the following questions:

- What did this project really cost?
- How many people did it really take?

- How long did it really take?
- When did people really start and when did they leave or stop?
- How much actual work did the team accomplish?
- What level of quality did the product achieve?
- How did cost and schedule estimates compare with the actual results?

I like to collect as much useful information as possible before the retrospective begins, but I don't expect miracles. I'm not looking for a Herculean effort from management or from team members who, while recuperating from the pressured end of the project, may resemble brain-dead zombies. I'm looking for coarse-grain data, something that can help with quick approximations, and one of my preferred pieces of data to collect is one I mentioned earlier—cost per line of code. For other types of effort data, I usually turn to the management team, the systems integrator, and the defects tracker.

The Management Team: Many of my questions can be answered by the management team. I ask managers to search through their records to come up with the most accurate numbers they have for cost, time, head count over time, and quality of work produced.

When preparing the management team for a retrospective, I discuss what questions we might ask project staff in order to obtain the most useful effort data. Every project is different, so there are no universally applicable data. Determining appropriate questions depends on such factors as the maturity of the team's process, the project's size, and the complexity of components (hardware, software, contractors, new technology, and third-party components, for example). Occasionally, managers will suggest collecting information that is impossible to get, but they usually back off when they realize that I'm expecting them to be responsible for obtaining the data.

The collection of management-oriented effort data seems to work best when one person is appointed to collect data about the whole project. This person can be a manager, but often someone who is interested in moving into management could be assigned the job as it provides a tremendous opportunity to learn about the details of managing.

Validation of future schedules is one reason I capture effort data, but I also want to see whether there are any interesting trends to investigate during the retrospective. Often when I contact a manager to find out how the data collection is going, I'm pleasantly surprised to discover that he or she has spent hours looking at many different aspects of the system, and has made some interesting discoveries.

With some clients, I discover that key project information is not available. This discovery tells me a lot about what kind of control these managers had over their project. During the retrospective, I raise the issue of data availability to see whether team members have ideas on how to capture better data on the next project.

The Systems Integrator: Usually, there is one person who stands out in a small group of people who can give a detailed view of the finished system through answers to the following questions:

- How many lines of code were built?
- How many routines were built?
- What were the sizes of the routines?
- What percentage of the code was acquired rather than built?
- Which routines had trouble going through systems integration?
- What patterns did you see?

The systems integrator, who also may be the person who directs the configuration management system, is the person who can answer these questions.

Sample Effort Data Collection E-mail

With the managers' approval, I introduce myself to this person on the phone and explain what information and data I hope to capture. I usually follow the phone call with e-mail to summarize what we have discussed. A sample e-mail follows:

Howdy Kyle,

As we discussed, Ellen Banks has indicated that you are the person to help me collect some effort data on the recent BIM project. Most software organizations have a long-term optimistic memory. This means a project from the past is remembered to be easier than it actually was. The end of a project is a perfect time to figure out how much effort really went into the project. This effort-data collection may aid project members in "learning what to do differently next time," but another benefit is a corporate memory of past projects. This corporate memory is useful as a reality check during future scheduling efforts. Comparing the expectations for the future against past projects is a good way to validate or question pending schedule plans.

Of course, sometimes this kind of information is just not available; in which case, we should have a discussion of what data we want to capture next time around. Here are some questions I'd like to pose to you. Please provide as much detail as possible.

1) What were the total number of lines of code produced in your project as reported by your compiler? (The compiler documentation might list lines of code as "program statements.")

2) What were the meaningful "chunks" of work for which we want to/can capture effort information? ("Schedule-tracked activity" is a good chunk. Other chunks include work done by the Red Team, by the Blue Team, or by each specific person. If possible, get the information by the schedule-tracked activity item on the schedule.)

3) How many lines of code were there for each chunk?

4) How does the effort spent on this project compare with a similar project?

5) In terms of "lines of code," what percent of code was not written from scratch and what effort did it take to incorporate this "foreign" code?

6) What was the calendar time and number of people required for each chunk? (This might be difficult information to capture. Sometimes, an activity changes over its life as people come and go. The chunk might have started out as one chunk and turned into three chunks, for example. The effort people put into that chunk might not be clear, because they "put in 60 hours per week." Do the best you can. If there are a great number of changes in the schedule, to the point

where it can't be tracked, then that is interesting to look at in the retrospective, and precise numbers become less important than discussion about what to do differently. Likewise, if effort is not clear, and over-work seems to be a major problem, we need to address this in the retrospective. Also, for each chunk, please get a count of how many schedule slips occurred—at least the important ones.)

I expect that you will be able to answer Question 1 fairly easily. It would be great if you can also answer Questions 2 and 3. The answer to Question 4 might be harder to get. Frankly, I'll be surprised if you can reconstruct enough information for it. Given the time frame until the retrospective, I doubt answers to Questions 5 and 6 are reasonable to expect, but please think about capturing whatever meaningful data you can.

By the way, I suggested the "lines of code" measure because compilers usually can answer that question. I know how inaccurate using such a metric is—so if you have a better metric, I'm open to it (for example, objects, use cases, or function points). What I'm looking for here is

- some measure of effort that the team can use to discover "interesting" things about this project
- questions that we know we cannot answer this time around, but that would be useful for us to have data about next time
- a demonstration that team members worked harder than they realize

These questions are guidelines. Brainstorm with your colleagues to formulate other interesting questions and then try to get answers. Let's talk on the phone and figure out what really makes sense after you have had a chance to think about this. I'll call you soon to see how things are going.

—Norm

I let the systems integrator or whoever is serving as data collector decide on the exact nature of the metrics he or she captures.

Determining the best metrics to use depends on the technology. For example, if the team has been using objects, then useful metrics might be

- number of classes
- methods per class
- number of class instantiations
- profile of inheritance structure
- number of library classes used

On the other hand, a relational-database-intensive or framework-driven project might call for very different metrics.

If the systems integrator is comfortable with public speaking, I ask him or her to prepare and give a verbal report to the retrospective community. Otherwise, I present the results.

The Defects Tracker: On a project, there is usually someone who runs the bug-tracking system and makes sure that defect reports get entered and processed through various stages. This defects tracker generates summary reports, and generally knows what bugs are unresolved and which ones are real problems. This person also knows a great deal about what kinds of defects showed up over the life of the project, which defects recurred, which ones were difficult to fix, and which were deferred to be fixed at a later time—and why.

I meet with the defects tracker, and together we explore what kinds of questions to ask and what kinds of data to collect. From this information, I can get a sense of the quality of the project by studying the defects. While doing this, I need to be very careful not to single out or embarrass anyone. If this happens, then the defects-tracking system will never again contain valid data. In addition, I ask the defects tracker a battery of important but sensitive questions, the answers to which will be kept between the two of us.

Some examples of basic questions include

- What was the total number of reported defects?
- How many defects were repaired?

- How many defects were deferred?
- What was the pattern of defects over time in relation to the major milestones?
- How many releases were tested?
- How much time was allocated to test each release?
- How much confidence did the testers have in each release?
- How much time was scheduled for testing and how much time did it actually take?

Some examples of more sensitive questions include

- How many defects were created by each group or person?
- How many defects were found by each group or person?
- How many defects were found by each kind of test?
- As you look at the defects data now, what interesting patterns emerge?
- Did the severity of deferred defects change as a function of time or because of proximity to a milestone?
- Did the severity of deferred defects depend upon who made the decision to defer?
- Did the nature of reported defects change as a function of time or project phase?
- Did the nature of reported defects depend upon who was doing the testing?

After the defects tracker has studied the collection of data on defects, we decide together what information should be shared publicly and what information needs to be handled more carefully. In deciding what to disclose, keep in mind the following:

We are not out to blame anyone. We assume that all group members did the best they could, given what they knew at the time. Our goal here is to learn how to do a better job next time. What is the best way to make this happen?

READY THE TEAM

We have detailed how to prepare the managers for the retrospective. Now, let's turn our attention to the team. Here is a review of the objectives that I, as a facilitator, want to pursue as part of the preparation effort:

- I want all participants to understand that a retrospective is a positive learning experience, not an opportunity for blame and counter-blame.
- I want participants to be confident that I will be able to lead this process, that I will understand the nuances of the discussion, and that I will provide a safe and confidential arena for them to talk about their experience.
- I want participants to be able to review the entire project. At the immediate end of a project, people can easily recall the prior few weeks, but the earlier months may be vague, at best. Participants need to review the entire project to be able to bring a complete perspective to the retrospective.

Three Sample Retrospective Handouts

In most instances, it is the managers who introduce the team to the idea of a retrospective. Since I am not usually on site at the time the retrospective is announced, I do as much as I can to help prepare the managers for the task. Some team members will find the thought of a review intimidating, and it's important that their introduction to the idea be handled well. The managers need to explain what a retrospective is, why they are doing it, and when it will be held. I provide them with three handouts to augment the announcement. The first is an informational sheet explaining what a retrospective is, the second is my biographical sketch, and the third contains questions for the group to consider before coming to the retrospective.

Besides describing a retrospective, the first handout sets the tone that recognizes that project members did the best that they could and explains what people need to do to get ready.

What Is a Retrospective? How Should You Get Ready?

In the movie *Dances with Wolves,* a tribe of Native Americans celebrates the success of a buffalo hunt by telling and retelling the story of the hunt around a campfire. Telling the story is a very important ritual because it provides a lesson for all the hunts to come. It is the way wisdom is passed on. In the software engineering field, a retrospective works much the same way—its purpose is to help you review your most recent project, in order to understand what happened, what worked well, and what to do differently next time. It is not an activity of finding fault with anyone, but rather an activity for learning from our experiences.

To have gotten your project to its current stage, you undoubtedly expended a great deal of effort and made many sacrifices. In a sense, the effort and sacrifice are the tuition that you paid. Now the question is, What did you learn? *Learning* is what this retrospective is all about: It is about improving your practice by reflecting on your recent experiences.

During the retrospective, we will review the entire project from many different perspectives, using as much factual information as can be discovered. The review is much like an archaeological research project in that we want to learn and remember, in part, by collecting and analyzing "artifacts" from the project. By artifacts, I mean memos, meeting notes, old schedules (all of them), calendars, white papers, budgets, project plans, personnel loading charts, and so forth. Artifacts can be anything that will remind you of what happened during the project and when it happened.

A key artifact is your calendar from the beginning of the project, so please bring it. (Reviewing your calendar should help refresh your memory and may provide clues about where else to find artifacts.) In addition to bringing the calendar, please search for artifacts in your desk, briefcase, old e-mail files, notebooks, bug status reports, old conference room schedules, notice boards, the recycle pile, and wherever else you can think of that might help document the project.

At this moment, you are probably worn out and getting away is most likely a higher priority than looking at your recent past. Take some time for yourself—it's important—and then please put some effort into this artifact dig. We want the next project to go better, and that will happen only if we learn from this one. There are two other reasons for putting effort into the artifact dig. First, we will analyze the artifacts to construct a time line of important events. Second, awards will be given for the most artifacts collected, the most creative or unusual artifact, and the most important artifact.

Please also answer the questions on the "Retrospective Pre-work Handout" and fax or e-mail it back to me. Your answers will help me get prepared, and might begin the review process for you.

Congratulations on getting to the end of the project! I look forward to working with you.

—Norm

Although each manager needs to announce the coming of the retrospective in his or her own way, distribution of my written explanation can reinforce the information that managers remember to convey to team members from their preliminary discussions with me.

The artifacts search I ask for in the handout makes the preparation a bit of a game and also encourages creativity. The best time for project members to begin the search is after the product has been released, but before the retrospective is held. The search has a beneficial side effect—team members clean up their desks! Let's face it—developers are usually too tired to do much of anything else at the end of a project, and so clearing their desks to uncover artifacts is a suitable activity.

The true importance of the artifacts search will be discussed later, but a simple, early justification for the activity is that as people look for these artifacts and recall the stories behind them, they begin the process of remembering, discovering, and learning from the project. The search for artifacts is a subtle but significant activity that is actually the beginning of the review.

The memo acknowledges the fact that project members have worked hard, are tired, and probably have a few more important things to do than getting ready for what they undoubtedly perceive as "more work." Giving them permission ostensibly to do something else (which is unusual in this business!) makes team members feel more relaxed, and frees them to search for artifacts in a leisurely, non-pressured manner. By this acknowledgment, I'm trying to establish a tone that says, "Whatever you can manage to do is okay."

For the second handout, the biographical sketch, I intentionally use a folksy style so that I look less like a snooty expert and more like a regular Joe. I usually tailor this handout to fit with the team's temperament and experiences as I understand them. The following sketch is similar to one I used with a team that was laid-back and a bit counterculture:

Who Is Norm Kerth?

I know there are a number of you whom I have not had the pleasure of meeting. I suppose you are wondering, "Who is this guy who is coming in to lead the retrospective?"

"After all," you may be thinking, "I heard he's over forty, never wears a tie, has a beard, and lives on a houseboat—but can he be trusted?"

Those details are true, but I guess I should tell you a bit more about myself. I graduated from Cal-Berkeley with a degree in EE and CS in 1974. While a student, I worked for Hewlett-Packard in Quality Assurance for the hand-held calculators division.

After leaving H-P, I spent ten years with Tektronix in Beaverton, Oregon, engineering software for test equipment, for integrated manufacturing test systems, and for embedded systems applications. Eventually, I moved to the research organization, to create, lead, and manage the Software Engineering Research Group. Our responsibility was to look at ways to improve software development. Issues we addressed included walkthroughs, methodologies, CASE tools, building reusable software components, object-oriented technologies, software-project scheduling, and effective software management.

I joined the faculty at the University of Portland in 1984, where I taught software engineering and operating systems courses. At the same time, I started my consulting practice, which I continue to this day. My goal in this consulting practice is to help companies get better at developing software on time, within budget, and in a manner that is both enjoyable and rewarding.

Oh, I guess I also should tell you that I am a Smalltalk bigot, but I recognize the fact that C++ and Java are here to stay. Frankly, I believe that which language you use is less important than your mastering the analysis, design, and quality-assurance processes.

I hope this answers a few questions about me. I look forward to trading stories about our experiences.

—Norm

The reason I tailor my description to fit the firm's culture is that doing so helps me establish myself as a "safe" person. If I am going to be an effective facilitator, the participants need to see me as a trustworthy, strong, and competent leader who is capable of keeping discoveries confidential.

My third handout asks each participant to answer, in confidence, questions that will help me understand goals as well as the concerns any participant might have about the retrospective. The answers tell me where to probe to uncover problems specific to the project.

Retrospective Pre-work Handout

November 30 to December 2, I will be working with your group to review what went on during the BIM project. As I explained in my "What Is a Retrospective? How Should You Get Ready?" handout, the goal of this review is to understand what happened, what worked well, and what to do differently next time.

To help me prepare for this retrospective, I have a number of questions that I would like you to answer. You can respond by sending me a letter, e-mail, or a fax.

Mail to:
Norm Kerth
P.O. Box 82907
Portland, OR
97282-0907

Fax to:
503-233-2163

E-mail to:
nkerth@acm.org

Your answers will be kept in strict confidence. I will review everyone's comments and discuss any patterns I see, but no individual response will be singled out.

So, here are my questions:

1. For us to learn the most from this experience, what topics need to be discussed?
2. What do you hope can happen for you during the retrospective?
3. What long-term impact do you hope this retrospective will have?
4. What reservations, concerns, or worries do you have about this retrospective?
5. What emotions do you feel as you think about this meeting?
6. What else should I ask and how would you respond?

So that I can do a good job getting prepared, I need your answers by November 25. I thank you in advance for your effort.

—Norm

The act of answering the questions posed in the "Retrospective Pre-work Handout" helps the team members to organize information they think is important—whether it pertains to dreams, hopes, or purely practical concerns. This activity may lead them to find the courage for deeper sharing during the retrospective because the tough issues will have already been expressed on paper, and therefore it may seem less scary to discuss them publicly. Furthermore, answering the questions may prompt some team members to share views with "safe allies" before the retrospective, thereby increasing the probability that important issues will be raised during the review.

WHEN TO GET THE LEGAL DEPARTMENT INVOLVED

In the early stages of preparing, make sure you ask whether there is any litigation pending on the project. It's a simple question, but the answer is very important if it is yes.

A True Story

I had a client who farmed out a major piece of work to a subcontractor. After months of craziness with nothing delivered, my client stopped the project and refused to make any payments to the subcontractor. Blame was high on both sides. A lawsuit looked very likely.

The subcontractor held a review of its portion of the project and delivered a less-than-honest appraisal of the situation to my client. Actually, the report was a whitewash carefully prepared by the subcontractor's legal department.

With my client, I set about to hold a retrospective to see what could be learned about the client company's interactions with subcontractors and about its own work. When my client's attorney learned of our plans to hold a retrospective, he used his authority as legal counsel to cancel it just as we were starting. We were shocked, but the attorney explained that if we had held the review, everything we wrote or said would become "discoverable evidence." The lawyers for the subcontractor would have had an easy job if we gave them a list titled "Things We Learned" and another one titled "What to Do Differently Next Time."

However, canceling the retrospective was not the end of the story. The attorney recognized the benefit of spending the next three days with all the participants on the project talking about what really happened. Up until then, he had only heard the story from senior management. As legal counsel, he requested that all participants convene to help him prepare for the case. All discussions were to be considered privileged communication between attorney and client and only the attorney could take notes.

We held the retrospective as we had planned, the only difference being that sessions were held exclusively in the presence of the attorney. The retrospective report was produced by the legal staff with the help of the participants. Neither the report nor the list of things learned could be shared with people outside the project until the litigation was concluded, and all documents generated for or during the retrospective were held confidential by the attorney.

In the end, the attorney discovered so many "smoking guns" that he could use in court that he was sure he could get the other side to back down. He was handed artifacts containing telephone logs of conversations proving cover-ups of poor quality, subcontractor memos explaining that it was "hacking junk and delivering it simply to solve an internal cash-flow problem," a written request from the subcontractor that my client's QA group "soften defect reports in order to assure that the project stay on schedule," and numerous other reports of points at which the specifications in the contract were not followed by the subcontractor. He had proof that the subcontractor had not used the methodology required by the contract.

The attorney's reaction to the retrospective was a glowing testimonial: "It was an amazingly efficient way to get prepared for my case. For once in my life, I felt I was getting an honest and complete picture of a situation. I think retrospectives might become a tool I use on even some of my toughest cases."

TRACK DETAILS WITH A CHECKLIST

Retrospectives are complex activities. To be successful, you need to focus your attention on the larger issues—the people, the story, and the process, and you may feel you don't have time to deal with the smaller details. Be forewarned, however, that a neglected detail can ruin a retrospective.

To prevent my overlooking something small but important, I've developed a checklist to remind me of the activities that need to happen but that I don't want to spend a lot of time monitoring. Every facilitator's checklist will probably be unique in some regard, but here's mine to use as a guideline:

Retrospective Checklist

- Five flip-chart stands with pads (or, one flip-chart stand and pad for every five attendees)

    When we break into sub-teams, each team will need its own place to work. Sub-team work will be centered around a flip chart. When we prepare the time line, we will be collecting information from five categories.

- 100 feet of butcher paper about 36" wide to use for the time line

    You can get this at most art-supply stores for about $.25 per yard.

- Five-to-six rolls of masking tape (or whatever adhesive the meeting-room owner prefers be used on the walls)

    Facility managers may have specific requirements for how they will permit paper to be hung on their walls. Find out whether hanging paper is an issue and what to do if it is. Make sure in advance that the room will have a space where the time line can be hung (30' to 50' long and 5' to 6' high).

- 1,000 5" x 8" file cards
- One 9" x 12" (or larger) envelope that can be used to save the "to do" lists
- Marker pens in a variety of colors, with at least one pen for each person
- One box of tissues
- One pair of scissors
- One package of note pads
- One box of pens
- Nametags
- Awards for the artifacts hunt and "Repair Damage Through Play" Exercise (such as certificates or trophies)
- CD Player and CD's (for music during the breaks)
- Instant camera and six packages of film (to record moments that should be remembered)
- A copy of this handbook (to refer to for ideas)
- VCR, television, and the videotape *Flight of the Phoenix* (to be used for the "Passive Analogy" Exercise)
- Instruction list for the manager of the facility to explain how you want the room arranged
- Copies of "Preparing a Proposal for Management"
- Select start and end times, and make sure you can have access to the room an hour before and after sessions are scheduled

    Some facilities prefer to control access to the rooms between sessions. Occasionally, this can become a serious problem. Also, consider how confidential this retrospective is and whether the room needs to be secure during off hours.

- Special-meals list; smoking and non-smoking room assignments

    Be sure the facility's manager knows in advance and is handling individual requests for room and meal preferences.

WHEN TO ARRIVE FOR THE RETROSPECTIVE

Although I always assign pre-retrospective work to the participants, only about 40 to 60 percent of team members actually complete the work. This is a fact of life, so I plan to arrive a day early to walk around the office, talk with individuals, and get a better sense of what occurred during the project.

For those who didn't do the pre-retrospective work, I let them know that I understand that they have other commitments, but I then say, "Now would be a good time for you to tell me your thoughts and any observations about the project." For those who did submit pre-retrospective work, I discuss it with them. They appreciate the fact that I have read their comments when they see my yellow highlighting marks. Occasionally, when an exceptionally good piece has been sent to me—a clever poem or song, for example—I ask the author whether I can share it with the rest of the participants. During this walk-around, I remind everyone about the hunt for artifacts, and generally let people get to know me. This getting-acquainted aspect may seem insignificant, but it is very important. It is during this time that I hear people's most private concerns.

Sometimes, participants want me to speak for them, to present the issues they are afraid to raise. I carefully explain that in my role as facilitator I will help get the story out, but I will not be a conduit for the anonymous submission of issues. I clarify that I do not know the whole background and cannot speak accurately for others, but that it is my job to find a safe way to allow issues to surface during the retrospective. I ask team members to work with me, but encourage them to share only what feels comfortable.

This kind of casual conversation can be very informative. If I hear about issues in confidence that do not come out in the retrospective, then I know the group has a problem sharing sensitive topics, and I will raise this as a major problem for the team to explore during the review.

CHAPTER SIX

Retrospective Exercises

Owl picked up Singed-Tail's copy of Swine in Wine *and quickly became intrigued. It wasn't the recipes themselves but the overall structure of the cookbook that caught his immediate interest. Leafing through it, he realized that the cookbooks he'd used had had the same structure as this book, with the first part including general information, the second part containing recipes, and the final section presenting special topics and suggestions on what the reader might explore next.*

It struck Owl that this three-part format let a reader browse while planning a menu. Although he knew that cookbook authors do not expect each and every recipe to be read or every dish to be prepared, he realized the value in a reader being able to look through all the recipes. Each cook is expected to use his or her own imagination, and to consider the guests' preferences, the available ingredients, the desired mood of the meal, and so forth, when choosing a menu. By using the cookbook author's ideas as well as his or her own preferences, the cook can design a perfect, unique meal for any situation.

This concept excited Owl. He thought back to the times that Bee or Ant or Singed-Tail had come to him for advice and had then commented on how much easier life would be if it came with instructions, just like a cookbook. At the time, he had wondered whether his friends were asking for a cookbook on how to live life, or for one simple recipe. He concluded that his friends were hoping for one single piece of advice that would guide them. But, as he had already explained to Bee after Bee's disastrous real-estate experience with Ant, "One size does not fit all."

Owl decided he would write a cookbook—one in which each "dish" would consist of a piece of sage wisdom. He would leave it up to the reader, however, to select the combination of dishes that fit the occasion.

Using Owl's insight and a modified cookbook approach, we can design retrospectives in which individual exercises are like dishes that make up a meal. In this chapter, I provide a variety of exercises. You can browse through these exercises while you think about how well one or another or a combination of several might fit your particular retrospective. In all likelihood, you will pick a few exercises and leave the remainder for other times. Or, you may wish to use an exercise of your own design or one which you discovered someplace else. Select each component to complement and support the other selections, not to duplicate or compete with them. Each exercise must add something unique to the retrospective and contribute to the whole so that the complete retrospective experience (rather than a single exercise) is remembered as a positive professional experience.

Like a meal, your retrospective can have a number of courses, with each one designed to accomplish certain goals and to prepare the participants for the next course. I typically divide retrospectives into three courses, which I call the Readying, the Past, and the Future. These courses are described in the paragraphs below.

The Readying: The Readying course prepares community members for exploration of what went on in their project. It provides an initial period during which I can convey my strengths as facilitator to members of the community: I demonstrate my confidence in them, my competence, my attentiveness, my willingness to understand their problems, my flexibility, and my ability to maintain any needed control. In this Readying phase, I want members of the group to

- build a trust-based relationship with me
- become convinced that the process is likely to have a positive outcome
- adopt an attitude that allows discovery, openness, curiosity, enthusiasm, and risk-taking
- participate in the design of some activities in order to build ownership
- establish safety measures to ensure that the truth and people's interpretations of events can be told without fear of retaliation
- design ground rules for behavior to be upheld throughout this retrospective

The Past: The purpose of this course is, literally, to dwell in the past, allowing individual team members to share their stories of the project and to help the group as a whole understand what really happened. Often, so much activity occurs during a project that no one person knows all that went on. During this part of the retrospective, members of the community can discover connections that they never before understood. They will have the opportunity to learn what the project really cost and how large it really was. They will be able to study the actual process, compare it with the intended process, and identify all problems. It is important to have everyone look at the damage that may have occurred to relationships and work to repair it. It is also important for members of the community to appreciate what was accomplished and to learn from each other through examination of their combined experiences. It's a chance to marvel at how much was learned during the past project.

The Future: The purpose of the Future course is to focus on the next project. In this activity, the team explores ways to use what individuals have learned during the retrospective in order to improve the next effort. The whole community participates in the planning discussion, not just the managers. Planning at this point is not project planning, nor product planning, but *process* planning. For many of the team members, this will be the first time they will have consciously thought about the processes they use.

Wait, read that last sentence again. "Consciously thought about the processes" is important because it is at this point that the magic of a retrospective occurs. After carefully considering all details of the previous project, everyone on the team will be ready to try new methods. This is a teachable moment, when people are ready to make serious commitments to change their work practices. The buy-in is there—that is, the collective understanding of what might happen if they don't change and the group's understanding of why change is necessary. This is the perfect time for a team to identify its own process and to work toward improving it.

The real power of a retrospective is in your hands during this Future course. Select exercises that empower the community to grow, dream, and act in ways that improve its work practice. As facilitator, you'll need to use subtlety at this point. Since the goal is to empower the community to do its own work better, then only gentle leadership is called for—you are giving the power back to the community. At the same time, you are still responsible for guiding the retrospective process. I find that my responsibility during this course involves listening first and then offering ideas to help people sell their vision.

THE EXERCISES

Now let's look at the exercises that make up the possible offerings for each course. In the remainder of this chapter are exercises for a retrospective. Chapter 8 contains additional exercises but ones which are to be used with groups that participated in a failed or canceled project. As you may have guessed, the exercises are depicted in terms of courses in a meal and are modeled on the cookbook format. Pick and choose for best results.

The Readying	The Past	The Future
Introduction	Artifacts Contest	Cross-Affinity Teams
I'm Too Busy	Develop a Time Line	Making the Magic Happen
Define Success	Emotions Seismograph	
Create Safety	Offer Appreciations	Change the Paper
	Passive Analogy	Closing the Retrospective
	Session Without Managers	
	Repair Damage Through Play	

THE "INTRODUCTION" EXERCISE

Course: The Readying

Purpose: This exercise is designed to welcome the group, set the tone for the retrospective, and briefly cover procedural items such as agenda, break times, use of facilities, and so on.

When to use: Once—at the start of the retrospective.

Typical duration: 30 minutes. This activity needs to be short! Get through your introduction to the events scheduled for the retrospective quickly but without seeming to hurry.

Procedure:

Step 1: Get off to a quick start. First impressions are important, so try to make the activities interesting from the start. Here's one idea: Begin the retrospective by asking people what the word "wisdom" means to them. Lead the discussion toward the understanding that wisdom is more than just *being smart* or *being educated*. Point out that elderly people are often believed to be wise. Why? What makes a 70-year-old person wise in comparison to a 19-year-old?

After the discussion has run its course, you may want to add your own observations. My view is that wisdom is the learning that comes from experience. I believe that each one of us can become wiser over time, but we do so only by learning from our successes and our failures. I see a retrospective as a chance to look back at what has occurred and to see what there is to be learned. I stress to team members that the goal is to capture the wisdom and lessons that are fresh in their minds from this last project.

If you think it will be helpful, give participants a copy of the "What Is a Retrospective?" handout presented in Chapter 5 of this book; stress again that this is not a hunt for the guilty. Introduce Kerth's Prime Directive:

Regardless of what we discover, we must understand and truly believe that everyone did the best job he or she could, given what was known at the time, his or her skills and abilities, the resources available, and the situation at hand.

Step 2: Be sure people have been introduced. If you haven't met everyone, or if you suspect all people in the room don't know each other already, this is the time to make brief introductions.

Step 3: Discuss the schedule and agenda. A well-run event requires a schedule and an agenda. This having been said, you need to have the flexibility to adapt the retrospective as it proceeds. Address the two topics separately, recording details of each on its own flip chart. The schedule will be precise on the start and stop times, meals, breaks, and so on, and the agenda will list a few items that give direction and order.

Step 4: Alert people to any idiosyncrasies about the facilities. If there is anything that needs to be communicated about the facilities, this is the time to mention it. For me, this has included warnings about rattlesnakes in the rocks out back or elk droppings on the front lawn. More typically, you'll need to provide directions to telephone banks and message centers, dress code details, earthquake safety procedures, or rules about tipping the staff. I usually ask one person to volunteer to act as our interface with the facilities staff. All requests should be funneled through this person so as to eliminate duplicated requests, conflicting messages, and problems of miscommunication.

Step 5: Provide the group with instant cameras. Memorable events occur during retrospectives. When possible, capture them in a snapshot. Hang the photos near the refreshment table or somewhere that the community is likely to gather. However, before you use a camera, check to see whether anyone objects to being photographed. If someone does object, discuss how to honor the objection while still leaving the group free to use the camera. The camera should be a resource for the entire community. Establish guidelines about camera protocol, as follows:

- If you see an event that would make a good picture, then grab the camera and take the picture.

- If you are worried about taking too many pictures, don't worry—there's plenty of film.
- If you end up in a photograph and are embarrassed, then please make the picture disappear.
- If you see any pictures that are especially meaningful to you, then feel free to take them home at the end of the retrospective.

THE "I'M TOO BUSY" EXERCISE

Course: The Readying

Purpose: Sometimes, people think they are too busy to participate in a retrospective, believing that the three days could be used for something more important than talking about the past. This exercise is designed to awaken the curiosity of reluctant participants and thereby to help them want to participate.

When to use: Use occasionally, but do use as needed. Determine the need during your site visit before the retrospective. Listen for comments that indicate that people are skeptical that this is a good use of their time.

Typical duration: 30 minutes.

Background and theory: There are four reasons most commonly cited by people resisting a retrospective:

1. They fear the retrospective process might become a witch hunt.
2. They had a bad experience with a poorly run retrospective in the past.
3. They experienced no positive changes in the workplace as the result of a previous retrospective.
4. They feel overworked and pressured, tending to measure results by how much activity they have engaged in, not by what they've accomplished.

The first three reasons are addressed in other exercises and are relatively easy to handle in a well-run retrospective. The fourth is more difficult to dissuade people of and is addressed here.

Procedure:

> *Step 1: Acknowledge that three days is quite a long time for people to be away from their responsibilities.* State that you understand that each person could accomplish a great deal on the job in that period of time. Rather than inviting discussion, pass out index cards and ask people to list what they would be working on if they weren't in the retrospective—in other words, ask them to make "to do" lists.

> *Step 2: Direct people to think back on the past project.* Tell them to count the number of days they felt were wasted because they didn't know something then that they now know. State, "I'm looking for rough numbers—just give me your best guess." Remain silent while they think through the project.

> *Step 3: Ask for a show of hands about the wasted days.* Pose the following questions, waiting to count hands raised after each question. "How many of you found no more than one day?" "How many found no more than three days?" and finally, "How many found at least six days?" Usually, no hands go up for the first two questions, but practically everyone shoots a hand up for the third. People almost always discover that there were more than six days wasted on the last project!

> *Step 4: Lead people through a simple financial projection.* Tell them, "If we spend the next three days learning what we can about this last project and if, as a result of what we learn, we can save at least six days on the next

project, that is a one hundred percent return on your company's investment. That seems to me to be a great return!"

Step 5: Build interest in the three-day commitment. Say, "I can easily show that we can find at least six days' savings on the next project. Actually, my experience tells me that we can find a great deal more than that." Ask each person to trust that the community will be able to accomplish this, but also ask people to confirm whether they believe this is a reasonable expectation. Confirmation is usually quick in coming, but be sure.

Step 6: Collect the "to do" lists. Pass a large envelope around the room and ask people to put their index cards in it. Reassure them, saying, "Don't worry, these lists aren't going away. I'll give them back at the end. By collecting the cards, I mean to show that for the moment we're putting this stuff on hold to see what we can learn." By the time you get to the end of the retrospective three days later, most people will have forgotten about their lists. During the closing, you can bring out the envelope and ask whether people want their cards. I find it interesting that few people care about their lists after the retrospective is over. In fact, it is common to hear people comment that the concerns expressed on the cards seem irrelevant given all that has transpired during the retrospective.

THE "DEFINE SUCCESS" EXERCISE

Course: The Readying

Purpose: At the end of a project, most team members remember their very recent struggle to get the job done. They are so focused on the problems they encountered that they are not likely to step back and appreciate what they have accomplished. Even with the most seriously failed project, there are things about which a team can be proud. With a successful project, there are also things that can be improved upon.

In this exercise, I attempt to establish the idea that the project's degree of success is not a relevant measure to use while people are trying to learn from their experiences. While not its goal, a benefit of this exercise is that it helps group members become comfortable with speaking openly—sharing what they think and having their opinions both heard and documented. They also learn to listen to other people's ideas, possibly discovering that they have allies in the group who share their views.

When to use: If the project was completed, always include the "Define Success" Exercise. If the project was canceled, turn to the exercises in Chapter 8 for help.

Typical duration: 30 to 60 minutes, depending on how long presentation of the effort data requires.

Procedure: Using a group-discussion format, start the dialogue by asking, "Was this project a success?" As group members talk, record the reasons people give for believing it was or was not successful.

Somewhere in the middle of the exercise, present the effort data collected before the retrospective. Reflecting on this type of data will help the group focus on the big picture.

Often, the project was more successful than anyone realized. In the software industry, we have so many failed projects that the act of completing a software system and delivering it to a customer is an accomplishment in and of itself. If the particular project my retrospective is reviewing did come to completion, I cite industry data (from Capers Jones or Barry Boehm, for example) to suggest that the project was more successful than 85 percent of similar efforts. I might say, "If I were grading on a curve, I would give any project that gets completed at least a B+ without knowing the details."

On the other hand, if the team insists on viewing the project as a failure, I let their truth stand. I then direct people's attention toward learning from this failure so that they never have to experience such a negative event again.

Regardless of how the group as a whole views the success of the project, I generally close this exercise by offering a final definition of a successful project:

> *A successful project is one on which everybody says, "I wish we could do that over again—the very same way."*

With this concept fresh in people's minds, I ask whether anyone thought the particular project met this definition. Usually, retrospective participants answer no. If that is the case, ask group members to think about what would have had to be different for them to answer yes. Then, ask them to take a few minutes to write down their thoughts.

This exercise will have been a success if participants have begun to give serious thought to what needs to be different, while considering what kind of project they would like to be a part of next time.

Background and theory: Effort data do not lie. When presented with effort data, people often discover that their impressions of the project have been wrong. Usually, far more work was accomplished than anyone realizes. Discovering this makes people curious about what other unexpected information might be learned during the retrospective.

The discussion of success establishes a precedent for talking openly about the project. The question posed is high-level and nonpersonal. Everyone has an opinion and can feel safe sharing it without the need to justify it. It becomes obvious that different opinions exist and all are to be tolerated. Also, the final definition of success sets a high standard for judging a project. It suggests that settling for less should be unacceptable. This idea may be novel enough to create even more group curiosity and enthusiasm.

The "Create Safety" Exercise

Course: The Readying

Purpose: At the beginning of a retrospective, people may have many fears that will prevent them from talking openly and honestly about the project. This exercise is designed to create a retrospective atmosphere that is safe, one in which team members can feel comfortable talking about important issues.

When to use: Whenever the practice of holding a retrospective is new. For teams in which a retrospective is common practice, safety may not be an issue. Make no assumptions and do some investigation before holding this exercise, but it's quite possible that safety was established in previous retrospectives, and that all the team members naturally expect this event will be safe. In these situations, the safety exercise can be skipped.

Typical duration: One to two hours.

Procedure:

> *Step 1: Make everything optional.* Stress that this process is not one of finding fault, but one of learning how to improve performance the next time. Establish that everything in this retrospective is optional by telling participants, "'Optional' means you don't have to par-

ticipate, you don't have to talk, you don't have to do any of the exercises that I assign. Each of you is the best judge of how you individually might acquire the most wisdom for yourself. I know that there may be moments when the most useful thing you can do is stay by yourself to sort issues out. I urge you to do whatever you need to do. The one thing I ask is that if you are not going to be meeting with us, just let me know beforehand." Ask everyone in the group to agree to this ground rule, including the managers.

Step 2: Take a poll of how safe people feel. Remark to the group that there are managers in the room, and ask whether people feel safe enough to say what needs to be said. Tell the group that you need to measure the level of safety in the room. By means of secret ballots, take a vote on safety, using a rating scale of 1 to 5, in which "5" means "Hey, no problem, I'll say anything." A vote of "4" means "I'll say most anything, but a few things might be hard to say." A mid-scale "3" means "I'll share some things, but keep a few things to myself." Lower down, a "2" means "I'm not going to say much. Mostly, I'll let other people bring up issues." Lowest on the safety scale, a "1" means "I'll smile, claim everything is great, and agree with whatever the managers say. No way will I let them know what I really think."

Collect the votes, mark them on a flip chart, and make a dramatic show of placing the ballots into a briefcase and locking the case. Usually, there are some people who do not feel safe and give a rating of "1" or "2." This is neither bad nor good. It's simply information about the team's interactions. I now try to change people's feeling of "safety" by letting them work in groups composed of people with whom they are used to working.

Step 3: Create natural-affinity groups. Tell the community that this activity is a "no-talking" exercise, saying, "In a moment, I'm going to ask you to stand up and move about. I want you to move near people with whom you have worked closely on this project and away from people with whom you worked very little. Besides the no-talking rule, one other rule is that you can only move yourself. Out of this, we will form groups that have a natural affinity to be together. Any questions?"

Once people begin to move, urge them to keep looking around to see whether this grouping is accurate; if not, tell them to move themselves to better reflect affinity. Eventually, the group will come to a rest although you might notice a person who can't stay put—he or she may have to shuttle between two or more groups. If this is the case, let it be, saying "Fine, it's part of the way this group works." Once people are settled, ask them to look around and comment on what they see. Ask the community to help you find the natural-affinity groups.

Next, send each group off to find a private space to discuss what can be done to make the retrospective safer. Ask people to take a flip chart and prepare a presentation to be made to the whole team. Tell them to "identify ground rules that would help, as well as other ideas that would increase safety."

After about thirty minutes, reassemble everyone, giving individual groups time to report their ideas. Working with the community as a whole, figure out how to incorporate each idea into the retrospective.

As ground rules are suggested, present them to the entire team for approval. If discussion occurs, modify the ground rule as needed. Write the ground rules on a flip-chart page, to be hung in a prominent place in the room.

Some possible ground rules can be

- We will try not to interrupt.
- We will accept people's opinions as neither right nor wrong, but just as opinions.
- We will speak from our own perspective.
- We will listen to everything someone has to say before we begin to develop a response.
- We will decide before we speak whether what we have to say is important enough to share at this time.

Every retrospective must include two additional important ground rules.

- All participation in the retrospective is optional.
- We will not make jokes about anyone in the room.

The final rule should be

- The ground rules can be amended after any break.

Besides establishing ground rules, the natural-affinity teams were asked to identify "other ideas that would increase safety." Sometimes, a team will suggest an exercise, such as the "Session Without Managers" Exercise described later in this chapter.

Step 4: Revisit the measure of safety. After setting the ground rules, take a second ballot to measure how safe people now feel. Hopefully, you will see a positive change. While it's nice if everyone in the room feels safe enough to vote "3" or above, that may not happen, as the situation described in the following True Story illustrates.

A True Story

I used to think I needed to get everyone up to a safety-level vote of at least a "3." My reasoning was that the team needed to be able to hear the full, uncensored story to make sense of the experience.

My view on this changed when I facilitated a retrospective in which one vote remained a "1" no matter what we did to improve safety. We spent a great deal of time on several rounds of votes and safety-work sessions—to no avail. Everyone was pretty frustrated, so I called for a break and asked people to write confidential notes to me explaining their feelings. Here is the message I got from the holdout:

I'M THE ONE.

I have a new job, and I'm not ready to announce it.

My goal here is to remain natural and noncommittal. I feel unsafe in that I have to keep this a secret for now.

I have no energy to work on this team's next project. I suggest that you give up on safety and move on.

With that experience, I discovered that a lame-duck employee can cause a real problem in a retrospective if I expect everyone to feel safe. In this instance, I was fortunate because this individual was willing to share his secret.

Now if one or two people still feel unsafe after the second ballot, then I acknowledge that their worry is a reality for this group, and tell people that I hope that individual feelings of safety will change as the retrospective progresses. I point to the one or two low marks on the flip chart and say, "That's a piece of information and we will see what comes up as we proceed. Just let it be for now." Then I move on.

On the other hand, if most members of the community do not feel safe, then the whole retrospective needs to be redesigned to deal with that issue. There is no reason to go on. No other valid data will come from the retrospective.

Another True Story

One retrospective community I worked with spent a great deal of time wording the ground rules just right. Fear was high, and trust among members of the community was low. The list of ground rules was the longest I'd ever seen. Finally, we got to a stage where everyone felt "safe enough" and we proceeded.

During the evening of the second day, I reflected on how well the retrospective was going and suddenly realized that many of the ground rules had been broken! The violations were subtle and, during the first day and a half of the retrospective, I hadn't noticed them. Faced with this realization, I imagined that a number of participants might be wondering why I had not commented on the ground-rule violations.

I decided to discuss the violations the next morning, and to begin to repair any damage that had been done by our disregarding the ground rules. I spent a restless night preparing to salvage what I could.

At the start of the third day, I reviewed the ground rules and asked the group to evaluate how well we were doing in maintaining safety and adhering to our rules. I took a third vote and was surprised by the results. The safety measure had gone up! By the last day, it seemed that the team understood that this was not a witch hunt, but a healthy review of the project. The small violations of ground rules were actually healthy signs that the team was comfortable with the retrospective.

Background and theory: I once asked retrospective participants to tell me what they were afraid of as we started the retrospective. They wrote anonymous notes on index cards and turned them in. Following are comments from individual participants:

- I'm shy in large group settings.
- I don't negotiate well on the spot. I need time to process. I fear I'm the only one who feels this way.

- Someone might get angry with me for what I say or think.
- I fear I might inadvertently hurt someone's feelings and damage future working relationships.
- If I express my opinions strongly, I may alienate myself from the team.
- My comments may affect the long-term impressions and perceptions people will have about me.
- The team will think I have a certain attitude.
- People may take offense at something I say. I especially worry when that other person is a manager.
- I fear the consequences for my family of me being fired because I spoke up.
- I fear the group will get sidetracked forever. We are very good at that.
- I fear being blamed for others' problems—becoming a target.
- My fear is being misunderstood and doing more damage than good to the team.
- I'm afraid of being tagged a candidate for "culling" because of disagreement with the approach being taken by management. If I disagree with the way the team is being built/organized, will I be trusted?
- I fear feeling inept and becoming a source of pain for the team.
- I fear looking stupid and not being taken seriously.
- I fear exposing myself to people I don't consider to be my friends.
- I fear long-term damage to my personal relationships, which may affect team effectiveness.

The fear people have of speaking the truth during a retrospective is real. However, while the feeling is justified, the actual danger may be far less than people imagine. The facilitator can help group members reduce their fear of speaking the truth by

- acknowledging that the fear is real
- letting people know that they are not alone in having this feeling

- addressing the specific fears
- asking each person to think of ways to establish a safe retrospective

THE "ARTIFACTS CONTEST" EXERCISE

Course: The Past

Purpose: In this exercise, members of the community use the collection of artifacts from the project to recall events that occurred during the entire life of the project. This activity triggers the process that ultimately will tell the full story of the project. The exercise usually brings out the point that no one person knows everything that went on during the project, and shows people that a retrospective can be fun.

When to use: Once during each retrospective.

Typical duration: One to two hours. (The amount of time needed will depend on how many people attend the retrospective.)

Procedure: The "What Is a Retrospective?" handout discussed in Chapter 5 instructed participants to search for artifacts from their project, and described a contest in which prizes would be awarded to whoever brought the *most* artifacts, the *most unusual* artifact, and the *most significant* artifact. The steps for this exercise follow.

Step 1: Discuss the artifacts. Ask the retrospective archaeologists to share and describe their artifacts. Then, ask them to place the artifacts on the floor in the middle of the room so that everyone can study the collection. For especially mysterious artifacts, encourage discussion of their significance, making sure the full stories are told. Ask questions about the artifacts as they occur to you and invite other people to raise questions, too—these questions, rather than being interruptions, help bring out the full story.

In some cases, I may be the only person who doesn't know the story, but having it told just for me is not a waste of time. The telling helps everyone in the community think back and remember events with greater clarity.

Step 2: Vote for the artifacts. After all the artifacts have been displayed and discussed, ask the retrospective participants to vote for the winners in the three categories. (I usually suggest that any given archaeologist should be able to win only once.) First identify the largest collection of artifacts, then vote for the most unusual artifact, and, finally, vote for the most significant one—that is, the artifact that is most important to understanding the project. Prizes for the three winners can be bottles of wine, funky hats, funny coffee mugs, or anything else you think will be especially appreciated by the specific community.

Most artifacts are documents. From among the multitudinous possibilities, someone usually produces a collection of all the product-development and delivery schedules, including the first schedule ever produced. If the first schedule is available, I usually ask permission to read it aloud. Invariably, as I read, the community as a body expresses amazement and even a bit of amusement at how optimistic—and naive—it was.

In addition to documents, there are artifacts that are objects. They can range from toys and automobile parts to dried bouquets and defunct computer components.

Throughout this exercise, the collection of artifacts piled on the floor grows. I am always impressed by the accomplishments these tokens represent, but participants in a retrospective also seem in awe when they see how much has been accomplished. As the exercise ends, I ask community members to quietly study the collection and reflect on all that it represents.

Step 3: Have the community arrange the artifacts and ask volunteers to take a few photographs. Save the photographs to post on the bulletin board or lay them out on a display table for future discussion.

Step 4: Collect the artifacts. To end this exercise, ask everyone to place the collected artifacts on a table that has been set up at the side of the room. Mention again that the artifacts represent valuable information, and suggest that people refer to specific artifacts throughout the retrospective for clarification or confirmation of project facts.

A True Story

Once, during the opening minutes of an "Artifacts Contest" Exercise, a contract programmer who had joined the project during the coding phase held up a notebook and claimed that it represented her nomination for "most significant artifact." She explained that because she usually joins projects late in the development cycle, she needs to be able to do her job without allocating any significant amount of time to learning about the project. She gets up to speed by understanding just the part of the system for which she will write code.

Holding up the notebook, she said, "This is the first project on which I've ever truly understood the whole system. It's because of this project notebook. It is complete, consistent, coherent, and correct. My nomination for 'most significant artifact' is not really this notebook, but its author—Michelle, our technical writer!"

As the contract programmer finished speaking, the room erupted in applause. Although Michelle had been assigned to the project full-time to keep the project records as well as to develop the users' manual, she had done much more for the project than perform just those two tasks. Her ability to find inconsistencies in the records and her tendency to keep asking questions until she understood the system caused the whole team to think, reflect, and rework.

When the votes came in, Michelle was named the team's most significant artifact, possibly making this retrospective the first time in history that a group of archaeologists considered a living human being to be their most precious artifact! (It might also have been the first time in history that a technical writer was recognized for what he or she contributed to a project!)

Background and theory: At the end of a yearlong or multiyear project, most team members clearly remember only the last few months of work. They need to think about and review the entire project before the retrospective begins. In truth, asking people to think back over the life of their project results in very little thoughtful recollection. However, the search for artifacts provides structure, and encourages people to think without the facilitator ever mentioning review as a goal. The artifacts search provides an unusual and fun way to stimulate important memories.

Making participants aware—in advance—of each of the three awards has its own purpose:

- Knowledge of a prize for "most artifacts" causes people to review all the documents that exist and thereby encourages them to think about the *entire* project. It also ensures that the group will have the documents needed during the retrospective.
- Knowledge of the award for "most unusual artifact" causes people to think about the project in creative ways and encourages them to develop meaningful stories about the unusual artifacts they are considering.
- Awareness of the "most significant artifact" category causes people to ask themselves what was most important during the project.

The collection of artifacts provides a way to ease participants into review of the project. Presentation of the artifacts establishes an atmosphere of fun and celebration. As the artifacts are discussed, participants realize that many events occurred without their awareness. This realization arouses a curiosity that usually carries into subsequent exercises. Since curiosity is a key to learning, this is a valuable exercise.

An additional benefit lies in the fact that the community itself votes on the awards, demonstrating that the team (not the facilitator) is in the position of deciding what is and what is not important.

References for Further Reading

Knowles, Malcolm. *The Adult Learner, A Neglected Species*, 4th ed. Houston: Gulf Publishing, 1990 (pp. 27–65).

Knowles provides a theoretical basis for the "Artifacts Contest" Exercise in this study, which investigates the way adults learn.

Shaffer, Carolyn R., and Kristin Anundsen. *Creating Community Anywhere.* New York: Jeremy P. Thurcher/Perigee Books, The Putnam Publishing Group, 1993 (pp. 305–19).

In this book, the telling of stories and the sharing of artifacts builds a community through a common experience.

Sawyer, Ruth. *The Way of the Storyteller.* New York: Penguin Books, 1942.

The power of storytelling as a time-tested way of learning and sharing experiences.

The "Develop a Time Line" Exercise

Course: The Past

Purpose: Building a time line allows each participant to add pieces to the collective story of the project. This exercise helps team members understand all that occurred during the project and enables them to build a disciplined framework for looking at the entire project in order to find the lessons that need to be learned.

When to use: Always.

Typical duration: Five to eight hours. (Spread this exercise over two days so that there is a night between for reflection.)

Procedure: This exercise is composed of two activities—the first is geared to building the time line, and the second, to mining the time line for gold.

121

Building the Time Line

Step 1: Prepare the room. First, cover one long wall with two rows of 36-inch-wide butcher paper. Make each row 30 to 60 feet long—the length will be determined by group size, project length, and available wall space. Divide the paper into meaningful time periods, moving chronologically from left to right. For example, for an 18-month project, time could be divided into quarters; for a half-year project, into six separate months.

Step 2: Ask community members to move into their natural-affinity groups. Once the groups are established, pass out a package of index cards to each group, along with marker pens. Each natural-affinity group should have its own color of pen.

Instruct each person to write his or her name on an index card, followed by the date he or she joined the project. If anyone participating in the retrospective left the project before it was completed, have that person make a second card stating name and departure date. Next, ask people to make cards for anyone missing from their team, giving specific names and start or departure dates. Explain how the time line works and ask people to tape their cards at the very top of the time line within the appropriate time period.

Step 3: Identify significant events. Ask each natural-affinity group to find a private space where people can work without interruption. Their task now is to identify significant events that occurred during the project, noting one event, with its dates, per card. Stress that this is not a *consensus* activity but rather is an *inclusive* activity. That is, anyone who thinks an event was important or significant should create a card for it.

Before groups begin the work assignment, ask people to look over their artifacts and take with them any artifacts that might help with this exercise.

Generating events cards often takes people quite a bit of time, because they find a great deal to discuss about the significant events. This period of reflection and remembering is an important benefit of preparing the cards. Allow one to two hours for this step.

Step 4: Reassemble the entire community. At the end of the allocated time, direct people to tape their date-bearing events cards on the wall-chart segment that corresponds to the correct time period. (When I started using this exercise, I tried to establish an orderly way of putting the cards up, but the participants always seemed to make it a free-for-all. Later, I realized that this unstructured session allows participants to post their cards anonymously. Now, I hand out many rolls of tape and tell everyone to "have at it.")

Step 5: Invite people to walk along the time line to see what strikes them. A special moment of learning happens after the time line has been completed. People are fascinated to see what they have created. Often, I need only announce a long coffee break and people begin walking along the time line on their own. Sometimes, I'll suggest, "Grab some paper and record your impressions." Some people study the time line individually, while others form groups to discuss their observations. Both approaches are fine; they just demonstrate differences in learning preferences.

Step 6: Leave the time line for a bit. You can expect the community to be tired at this point; it might be late in the afternoon of the first day or approaching lunch on the second day. A respite of some kind is in order. If a break is scheduled, adjourn until the next meeting time. If a break is not timely, shift into another exercise and return when the community is rested. I usually consider using the "Offer Appreciations" Exercise or a form of the "Repair Damage Through Play" Exercise (both are discussed in this chapter). Return and begin the "Mining the Time Line for Gold" activity after the community has had some rest.

Mining the Time Line for Gold

This second portion of the time-line exercise provides participants with a significant opportunity for learning because it forces a review of the project from a big-picture perspective. The time line depicts events deemed important from everyone's point of view; by mining it, people review the project, period by period, to see what associations, patterns, or anomalies can be discovered. The "gold" is the understanding that comes to group members as they look at the time line and discover they can learn more by working together than any one individual could have learned on his or her own.

Step 7: Put five flip charts on easels located around the room. Explain to the community, "This is where we will place our gold as we mine the time line. Each flip chart will contain a different kind of nugget." I label the flip charts with the following topic headlines:

- What worked well that we don't want to forget
- What we learned
- What we should do differently next time
- What still puzzles us
- What we need to discuss in greater detail

I use these five topics to help focus discussions as the time line is mined. Most of these topics are self-explanatory, but a few need elaboration.

The what-worked-well-that-we-don't-want-to-forget topic is phrased in a very particular way. Simply asking for what worked well can turn into a long list of motherhood-and-apple-pie statements. I'm looking for just those things that are at risk of being lost.

The what-still-puzzles-us topic encourages honest discussion about what the team doesn't know how to do. Such discussion often leads to training, invention, research, and discovery during the next project.

The what-we-need-to-discuss-in-greater-detail topic is used to keep the retrospective moving. During a discussion, if closure seems difficult, it is usually because the subject matter is complex and involves the melding of a number of viewpoints. I add the topic to the flip chart, explaining that we will return to it later in the retrospective.

One clear benefit of listing these last two topics is that they serve as a bridge from one course of our retrospective meal to the next—the activity of specifying puzzles from the past and identifying complex issues needing further discussion leads to planning for the future.

Step 8: Ask volunteers from the community to serve as recorders. Assign one volunteer to each flip chart. I delegate this task to volunteers rather than handling it myself because no one person can facilitate well and also act as scribe.

Step 9: Examine each time period in chronological sequence. To help people identify critical events, ask a variety of questions, such as

- What card jumps out at you as the most significant?
- What card surprises you?
- What card or cards don't you understand?
- Do you see any patterns emerging as you compare cards?
- What card should we discuss next?
- Is there another card suggesting this topic but from a different point of view?
- What card still needs discussion?

Use these questions to stimulate discussion. Once started, let the dialogue take its natural course but guide the discussion to formulate statements that can be written on one of the flip charts.

A True Story

During the closing hours of one retrospective, the group's vice president of software development visited us. His curiosity about the retrospective was refreshing, and although I gathered that the cost of the retrospective was a serious expense for him, he was most supportive and willing to help in any way he could.

As team members explained what they had accomplished during the three days, the VP became especially interested in the time line. He asked what would happen to it when we finished. Since we had already mined all the gold, I told him that we would probably throw it away. "No, please don't. I need it!" he replied. He went on to explain that his field was not software but water-distribution engineering (the firm produced software to control large water-flow systems). He said he had never realized how complex a software project was. The retrospective time line made it clear.

"Next week, some of my people will be making a pitch to our Board of Directors, hoping to establish a software-engineering process group. Frankly, I haven't been able to support them. I didn't understand why it was important. I want this time line in the boardroom. It communicates instantly what goes on in our company. It's real-life, not theory. This shows me that building professional software is much more complicated than what we were taught in my college courses. Now I finally understand why we need a software-process group."

The time line was installed in the corporate boardroom and remained for nearly a year. I gather it was the stimulus for many useful discussions about the discipline of building software, using terms that describe the way engineers control water.

THE "EMOTIONS SEISMOGRAPH" EXERCISE

Course: The Past

Purpose: On some projects, events cause unexpected changes in emotions. In this exercise, which is adapted from one I learned from my colleagues Jean McLendon and Eileen Strider, we explore the events that trigger emotional reactions. Our goal is to build better understanding.

When to use: I use this exercise on occasions when information submitted as pre-work indicates that there were numerous changes made during the project, and the people who made them (possibly the managers) didn't appreciate the impact those changes would have on the emotional health of the community. A fellow facilitator, Esther Derby, always uses the seismograph as part of the "Develop a Time Line" Exercise. For her, the seismograph is the key guide during the "Mining the Time Line for Gold" activity.

There are several points at which you might ask the community to draw a seismograph: For example, you might suggest this exercise after the group has had time to reflect on the time line, or perhaps at the beginning of the next day, or even at the end of the "Mining the Time Line for Gold" activity. I'd like to be more precise, but it is a decision based in large part on intuition.

Typical duration: One to two hours.

Procedure: This exercise uses the developing time line, and can be executed concurrently with the "Develop a Time Line" Exercise.

> *Step 1: Modify the time line.* Draw two parallel, horizontal lines, one foot apart on the butcher paper taped to the wall. These lines should be drawn to form a band running from left to right near the middle of the paper. During the "Building the Time Line" activity, the Step 4 instruction to community members to tape their events cards outside of the middle band, either above or below.

> *Step 2: Ask people to walk along the time line from left to right, reading the cards and drawing a continuous line in the middle band area.* The line should rise and fall to reflect

the feelings individuals had during the project at the time noted on the cards taped above. I usually explain the scale by saying, "A line within the top area of the band means 'This job is great! I can't wait to get to work.' One at the bottom means, 'I hate my job.' A line drawn in the middle means 'Hey, it's a job.'" Make sure each person uses the color marker pen that others in the same natural-affinity group are using.

The wording you use to give directions should be compatible with the cultural preferences of the group. Some groups are not comfortable talking about their feelings; others see a discussion of feelings as a natural part of their work. Depending on the group, I might ask people to rate either their "job satisfaction" or "the intensity of their feelings," or I might just say, "Mark what was going on for you at that point in time."

Just as you did in the "Building the Time Line" activity of the "Develop a Time Line" Exercise, tell the group to "have at it." Make sure this moment is a bit chaotic to assure a degree of privacy for anyone who wishes it.

Step 3: Help participants interpret the seismograph. To guide the interpretation of the seismograph, you have two choices. Either you can ask the community "What do you make of this?" and allow people to select points in time that they want to discuss, or you can note interesting trends and ask people to discuss them.

Background and theory: It is hard to initiate a discussion of feelings in the workplace, but once started, comments seem to flow easily. This exercise is designed to slowly move the community into that discussion. The seismograph allows feelings to stay private but shows—by the color of marker pen—whether various members of each natural-affinity group experienced the same feelings.

The discussion of feelings shows team members that they are not alone. It also gives them a way to talk in terms of the group's feelings while really discussing their own. As the discussion proceeds, individuals can shift from talking about the group's emotions to talking about their own.

THE "OFFER APPRECIATIONS" EXERCISE

Course: The Past

Purpose: This exercise provides an opportunity to give recognition to everyone who deserves it. On every project, there are heroes. In fact, usually everyone on the team performs some heroic act, at one time or another, that helps get the software out the door. However, as a culture, we seem to have lost the inclination to give someone a "high five" or say "great job!" As a result, individuals who singly or collectively perform great feats of heroic behavior remain unappreciated.

When to use: Use this exercise to take a break from the "Develop a Time Line" Exercise, at the end of the day when everyone is tired, or when something happens in the retrospective that suggests the community could benefit from this exercise (for example, you could introduce the exercise when you notice a few people sneaking in compliments during one of the other exercises). I use this exercise in about half of the retrospectives I facilitate.

Typical duration: One hour.

Procedure: Start this exercise by asking people to contribute to a definition of the word "hero." I usually look for a definition indicating some or all of the following characteristics:

> *A HERO IS... One who is endowed with great courage and strength, who is celebrated for bold exploits, and who is favored by the gods. ...One who is noted for feats of courage, especially one who has risked or sacrificed his or her life. ...One who is noted for special achievement in a particular field. ...One who has discovered and shared new knowledge, understanding, or inventions.*

Ask whether there were any heroes on the project. You will usually get a few nods. Discuss the fact that the phrase "great job!" is rarely spoken in our business, and then explain the exercise by saying, "You see hero worship and recognition of achievement all the time in the sports world. The fact is, giving a compliment feels great, and doesn't cost anything. On this project, everyone has had to do something significant to get the product out the door—and everyone needs to be acknowledged for that. I'd like this group to try the 'Offer Appreciations' Exercise. This is how it works: Someone who has an appreciation for another person will start off as 'It.' The person who is 'It' selects a hero, says the hero's name, and gives the appreciation. The message must be in the form of 'Tom, I appreciate you for...' "

Often, people will try to change the phrase into "I appreciate Tom for..." This use of the person's name as the object of the verb does not have the same impact as does direct salutatory address—so, interrupt and help the speaker rephrase the message.

For some people, it is very hard to receive a compliment. Encourage them to just listen to the message. If they want to say "thank you," that's fine, but they need not say anything else.

Once the appreciation has been delivered, the receiver of the appreciation is now 'It' and can offer an appreciation to someone else. This goes on until everyone has been the receiver at least once.

End this exercise by observing that it really does feel good to receive "appreciations." Giving one is a gift that costs nothing and means so much to the receiver. I tell the group that each of us is likely to think of more appreciations over the course of the retrospective as well as after our gathering. I encourage group members to share their appreciations as they come up. Then, I suggest that offering appreciations might be a good thing to add as an ongoing daily practice so that it becomes part of the group's culture.

As described in Chapter 2, there are times when a manager wants to give an appreciation to everyone. If this happens, let it. It would be unfair and unwise to restrict a manager to an appreciation of only one person. Occasionally, I change the exercise to let people volunteer appreciations as they feel the need. The "It" game is used to get things started, but it can be adapted to fit the mood of the retrospective.

Theory and background: The fundamental goal of a retrospective is change. Virginia Satir studied how to help groups change and developed a six-phase model that includes making contact, validating, creating awareness, promoting acceptance, making changes, and reinforcing changes.

The second phase—validating a person's self worth and willingness to consider the possibility of change—is built upon a foundation of offering a person honest expressions of appreciation. That is, appreciation for what the person has accomplished, what he or she has contributed or knows, or simply for who he or she is.

References for Further Reading

Loeschen, Sharon. *The Magic of Satir: Collected Sayings of Virginia Satir.* Long Beach, Calif.: Event Horizon Press, 1991 (pp. 7–15).

Loeschen provides an insightful discussion of Satir's use of appreciation in this inspiring collection. My entire work on retrospective rituals could have been derived from the Satir Change Cycle described in Loeschen's book.

THE "PASSIVE ANALOGY" EXERCISE

Course: The Past

Purpose: This exercise is designed to help people learn about their project by encouraging them to relax and let their minds wander while they enjoy a movie. The activity should be structured to offer entertainment that both provides parallels with the team's project and that enables group members to view the project from a different perspective.

When to use: I save this exercise for residential retrospectives. It fits best on the evening of the first day. It usually follows the "Building the Time Line" activity.

Typical duration: Two and one-half hours to watch the movie, with an additional one to two hours for discussion on the following morning, depending on the community's needs.

Procedure: Find a casual setting for community members to use that's different from their regular workspace. A room with a large-screen TV/VCR set-up, comfortable couches, and overstuffed chairs would be a good choice. Arrange to have snack food and soft drinks available.

Choose the movie that you feel most closely parallels the project you are facilitating. I almost always choose *Flight of the Phoenix,* featuring Jimmy Stewart and three co-stars. The plot of this movie, which revolves around the reassembling of a plane from scattered pieces of wreckage after a crash, provides an excellent analogy for most software projects.

Before showing the movie, instruct people to watch it while keeping in mind the context of their own project. At the end of the movie, ask everyone to consider questions such as the following for discussion the next day.

- How were events in this movie similar to those in your project? How were they different?
- What mistakes did the characters make that you avoided? How did your project avoid them?
- What did the movie characters do that you wish had been done on your project? How could their success have been experienced on your project?
- With whom in the movie did you most closely identify? Why?

By allowing people to "sleep" on these questions, you afford them the opportunity to process their ideas subconsciously. For many people, powerful insights come while they sleep.

To start the morning session on the next day, open the floor to a discussion of the questions. Use discussion of the next-to-last—which characters did people most identify with?—to set up the morning's final activity before lunch. People usually mention four characters after viewing *Flight of the Phoenix*. For the final activity, ask the participants to move into groups, one for each of the identified characters. Direct all who identified with the pilot in *Flight*, for example, to move to one corner of the room, those who identified with the character of the navigator, to a second corner, and so on. Next, give all four groups the same assignment, designed to help them uncover preferences in their problem-solving styles. Choose the assignment according to what you learned from the pre-work handout. Here is an example:

> *Think about what mistake your character made with which you have some personal experience. Did others in your group make this same type of mistake? Discuss how you can prevent such mistakes from occurring during future projects. Once you have identified a pattern, select a representative to report back to the whole community on your group's discussion and/or discovery.*

Background and theory: In *Flight of the Phoenix*, the four main characters typify problem-solving behaviors that correspond to the four temperament types in Keirsey-Bates theory. That is, people have certain preferences in the way they work to solve problems. Fundamental to Keirsey-Bates theory is the premise that people must learn to appreciate both their own preferences and also the preferences of others who use different problem-solving approaches. Through understanding of these differences, teams can preserve their diversity while still honoring the preferences of others and taking advantage of their strengths. The following chart identifies the temperament type of each of the four characters in the movie and describes problem-solving styles.

Movie Role	Type Identifiers (Keirsey-Bates)	Description of Preferences	Strengths
Pilot	Troubleshooter (SP)	Relies on the five senses for collecting information; prefers to make decisions on the spur of the moment.	Particularly strong at solving problems in a crisis.
Navigator	Facilitator (NF)	Relies on intuition for information; likely to consider the people element in making a decision.	Effective at forming and maintaining a team of collaborative individuals.
Army Officer	Industrialist (SJ)	Relies on the five senses for collecting information; prefers to make decisions rapidly.	Masterful at managing time and resources.
Airplane Designer	Scientist (NT)	Relies on intuition for information; uses logic and abstract thinking in making decisions.	Capable of establishing a conceptual perspective and mastering the complexities necessary to achieve a goal.

If participants are not familiar with type identification, summarize the technique in your own words but make available reference copies of the six books listed in the following "References for Further Reading." Do not insist on use of exact Keirsey-Bates terms but rather help people understand and verbalize their preferences. By asking people to select the character they most identify with, you help them articulate their temperament types and preferences. At this point in the exercise, you should be sure everyone in the group has a clear understanding of type differences. Guide type identification by asking questions such as the following:

- How did your character contribute to the team in a positive way?
- What weaknesses did your character have?
- What didn't your character appreciate in each of the other characters?
- What should your character have done differently?
- How do your answers reveal opportunities to change, modify, or preserve the way you function at work?

References for Further Reading

Keirsey, David, and Marilyn Bates. *Please Understand Me: Character & Temperament Types,* 4th ed. Del Mar, Calif.: Prometheus Nemesis Book Co., 1984.

Type preference theory is a powerful facilitator's tool, and it is clearly presented in this excellent work. We revisit this material in conjunction with the exercises detailed in Chapter 9.

Myers, I.B. *Gifts Differing.* Palo Alto, Calif.: Consulting Psychologists Press, 1980.

This is *the* seminal work and should be read by all facilitators.

Weinberg, Gerald M. *Quality Software Management, Volumes 1–4.* New York: Dorset House Publishing, 1992–1997.

> The Weinberg series provides much that is valuable on types and temperaments. See especially Appendix F in *Volume 4,* which gives a concise but clear summary.

THE "SESSION WITHOUT MANAGERS" EXERCISE

Course: The Past

Purpose: The purpose of this exercise is to help workers learn how to express their opinions honestly when they talk to management. In some environments, there is an "us versus them" attitude dividing managers from workers. Workers fear reprisal if they tell a manager what they think. Participants from such an environment are likely to begin the retrospective feeling oppressed and powerless. If you believe this to be the case from your review of the "Retrospective Pre-work Handout" or from initial interviews with project members prior to the start of the retrospective, then this exercise is a possibility.

When to use: I use this exercise infrequently and only when project members have tried to establish a safe retrospective environment, but have been unable to do so. The "Session Without Managers" Exercise is especially useful when the managers indicate that they want to hear what their workers have to say, but are frustrated because their people either don't communicate or communicate ineffectively. By holding the "Session Without Managers" Exercise, you encourage healthy dialogue. (If I have determined during the retrospective-preparation stage that the managers are not interested in such a dialogue, I generally decline to hold the retrospective at all!)

Schedule this exercise to be given after the "Develop a Time Line" Exercise but before any of the exercises that belong to the Future course. While various issues will arise during the time-line activities, this exercise will help identify the few sensitive issues that are not explored during the "Mining the Time Line for Gold" activity.

Typical duration: Two to three hours, depending on the magnitude of the problem, the amount of instruction you need to provide, and how complex a message is developed during the exercise.

Background and theory: When workers are afraid to tell managers what they think despite the fact that managers want the feedback, there may be a variety of dynamics at work.

Reluctance to speak freely may result from a worker's painful experiences with past managers. People who have picked up coping habits from previous work situations may carry those habits unknowingly into new relationships, even though the behavior is no longer needed.

A second dynamic may be a worker's perception that the manager is playing the same role as an authority figure from his or her childhood: a parent, a teacher, or a school principal, for example. In this situation, the worker may use response tactics learned as a child. You might see such a person exhibit childlike behavior, such as becoming tongue-tied or uncharacteristically quiet; or the person may exhibit fast, shallow breathing or show a marked change in posture.

Conversely, responsibility for a lack of communication may lie with the manager who may have responded to feedback in the past in a way that discouraged future input. Perhaps the manager frequently interrupted the worker to point out that something was wrong, or perhaps the same manager failed to respond in any way to the worker's input. Both scenarios can be fatal to open communication, but they do happen. Managers have a different perspective on the project and the company than workers have; they experience different pressures and difficulties, and they function in a world of budgets, office politics, and customer relations. Workers exist in a world of directives, schedules, and deadlines. Because both groups see events from such different viewpoints, either group may dismiss the other's message as invalid.

Another dynamic barring effective communication may be a manager's belief that he or she, as a leader, must have a solution to every problem. This expectation leads either to quick-fix solutions or to explanations of why things can't change. Both of these reactions prevent people from really listening to other people's ideas.

If any of these dynamics exist, they need to be addressed during this exercise. The key to opening channels for communication is helping the manager to understand that workers usually do want to be heard and that they don't expect all problems to be fixed.

Procedure: Send the managers off to meet with each other to consider everything they have heard so far. Ask them to develop a statement summarizing their view of what happened on the project and specifying what they believe should be done differently next time. Remain with the group of non-managers, and work with them to develop a similar message to managers. If there are two facilitators, the second one should work with the managers. Do *not* divide the group of non-managers into two groups as you want a single message or statement to be developed.

Step 1: Check safety. Once the managers have separated from the workers, perform a quick safety-check to see whether the workers once again feel safe enough to discuss issues. You may have to get everyone to agree that what is said in this meeting stays in this meeting.

Step 2: Direct the workers to develop a message for their managers. The workers' message is to follow a specific format:

- The message should not be a list of complaints. It might start as that, but every negative issue raised needs to be paired with a positive recommendation.
- The message should explain why its authors believe this can be a "win-win" situation for all involved, indicating they've made every effort to see the problem from the managers' side as well as from their own side.
- The message must communicate a strong commitment to helping the managers do a better job.
- The message needs to show that the workers are ready to share in the responsibility of moving with the managers toward the solution.

As facilitator, your role is to empower the workers to speak for themselves. Resist intervening unless people are no longer making progress. If you do need to take

141

the lead, try to yield that job to the first capable person who appears to be moving into a leadership role.

Be prepared to help non-managers reshape conflicting, incongruent messages into congruent, harmonious ones. Try to do this from a collaborator's position rather than from a facilitator's position.

Step 3: Reassemble everyone once the managers and the workers have both developed their messages. I use the following approach for delivery of the two messages.

- First, instruct workers to deliver their message completely. Managers can ask questions related to clarifying the message, but they cannot comment on it until the message has been completely delivered.
- Next, ask managers to comment on the message, either immediately or at a later, mutually agreeable time. If at all possible, they should communicate their response during the retrospective so that you, as the facilitator, can guide the exchange.
- Then, give managers the opportunity to deliver their message. Workers can ask questions related to understanding the message, but, like the managers, they cannot comment on it until the message has been completely delivered.
- Finally, encourage workers to respond to the managers' message.

As facilitator, I prefer to have one or more workers deliver the message to the managers; I agree to serve as spokesperson only as a last resort. My reason for staying away from this role is that I don't have the context of experiences shared by the people on the project, and therefore cannot explain the message as well as they can. If no worker feels safe enough to deliver the message, I preview the content with the workers, asking them to provide verbal context and detailed explanation. Whoever seems most able to help me with the explanation usually becomes the person I will eventually ask to take over for me (again, my goal is to empower the workers).

A final note: The cartoon near the beginning of this exercise suggests an unpleasant situation. A workplace in which managers and workers are not in continuous effective dialogue is not a healthy one. The "Session Without Managers" Exercise provides a stepping-stone toward helping the community find a better way of working. Whenever this exercise has proven necessary, I follow it up with a worker-management communication-improvement activity in the Future course, usually as an item to be broached in the "Cross-Affinity Teams" Exercise.

References for Further Reading

Satir, Virginia. *The New Peoplemaking*. Palo Alto, Calif.: Science and Behavior Books, 1988.

> Written for lay people, Satir's work provides a good introduction to the topics of communication stances and rules. See especially Chapters 6 through 9.

_____. *The Satir Model: Family Therapy and Beyond*. Palo Alto, Calif.: Science and Behavior Books, 1991.

> This book is intended for professionals in the field of therapy, but it can be quite enlightening to facilitators. Chapters 3 and 4 treat stances and congruence in greater detail than the topics are treated in *The New Peoplemaking*.

Seashore, Charles N., Edith Whitfield Seashore, and Gerald M. Weinberg. *What Did You Say? The Art of Giving and Receiving Feedback*. Columbia, Md.: Bingham House Books, 1991.

> Now available directly from the authors—see www.geraldmweinberg.com for details—this compelling book explores the art of giving and receiving

feedback, presenting the theory upon which the "Session Without Managers" Exercise is designed.

THE "REPAIR DAMAGE THROUGH PLAY" EXERCISE

Course: The Past

Purpose: During a project's final days, everyone experiences a great deal of stress, and relationships between workers may become damaged. This exercise is designed to repair that damage by creating opportunities for people to play together. Playing time gives all participants a chance to release tension and to reflect on what they have discovered during the retrospective.

When to use: Daily, up to several times a day for residential retrospectives. It is effective to use evenings, after lunch, or whenever the community needs a break.

Typical duration: One hour or longer.

Procedure: This exercise is not one specific activity, but rather includes a variety of activities held as needed throughout the retrospective. The events range from unstructured, informal activities to well-organized games. I like to include both.

For unstructured activities, I give directions such as, "All of you have been indoors too long. Take your natural-affinity team outside and find something to do. Don't talk about the project for at least thirty minutes. Let's reconvene in an hour."

Group members might go for a walk, take a bike ride, or simply sit on a park bench. They might explore the neighborhood, practice juggling, or just watch the clouds float by.

Structured activities usually involve playing games with rules, requiring people to interact with each other. Games afford opportunities for people to team up, either within natural-affinity groups or as non-affinity groups of people who don't usually work together. Activities can range from pool, Ping-Pong, and poker, to touch football, tennis, or Pictionary. I ask members of the community to plan these structured, recreational activities because people tend to benefit more from recreational activities they've chosen than from activities assigned to them. The process of working together to prepare food also provides an important bonding experience. People who plan, shop for, and cook out at a barbecue, for example, can become better teammates. Active participation in the preparation of a shared meal generally builds powerful team connections.

To motivate people's participation in structured "play" activities, I bring to each retrospective an old trophy that I usually have been able to find at a flea market or in a consignment shop. To illustrate that this trophy is special, I tell some story that is too crazy to be believed, but which contributes to making the trophy prized by members of the community. Teams compete for the trophy in a variety of activities so that all individuals have the chance to demonstrate their particular skills. When I award the trophy, I explain, "This trophy is to become a continuous-challenge trophy, with the rules to be defined by you." I give some examples of how people can continue to use the trophy on future projects, such as competing for the trophy only at the end of projects or only in sports that they have never played together before—the sillier the better.

Background and theory: When a team goes through difficult times on a project, no one enjoys the experience. Stress and tension are high, and people behave uncharacteristically. In such circumstances, it's easy for team members to dislike the experience so much that they will decide to leave the team. However, a community that plays together will form special bonds. The relationships built around these play-filled times help individuals find new reserves of strength and patience to carry them through the hard times.

If you are facilitating a retrospective for a team whose members are already in the habit of playing, then this exercise provides a good opportunity for them to further strengthen their relationship. Through play, damage that occurred from end-of-project stress begins to repair itself. People see each other as individuals rather than just as barriers to progress or as reminders of problems.

THE "CROSS-AFFINITY TEAMS" EXERCISE

Course: The Future

Purpose: In the "Mining the Time Line for Gold" activity of the "Develop a Time Line" Exercise, issues were identified that required further discussion. In most cases, these issues will have emerged from a variety of viewpoints, usually representing the specific orientation or interest of the separate natural-affinity teams. In the time-line exercise, the community also identified topics that were puzzling. This "Cross-Affinity Teams" Exercise is used to further those discussions, by breaking the community into different subgroups. The goal is to identify better ways to direct the next project.

When to use: Always.

Typical duration: Five to six hours.

Procedure: This exercise uses two of the five flip charts created in the "Develop a Time Line" Exercise. Pick the charts labeled "What still puzzles us" and "What we need to discuss in greater detail."

> *Step 1: With the community, review the topics listed on the two flip charts.* Ask people to help you clarify, organize, and consolidate entries; then list the issues in order of priority. Identify the three or four issues that people agree most need to be discussed at this point in the retrospective.

> *Step 2: Build teams consisting of at least one member from each natural-affinity group.* These cross-affinity teams will be assigned responsibility for exploring one of the three or four issues identified above.
>
> Team makeup is important: When composing cross-affinity teams, you, as facilitator, may need to make several decisions. For communities in which managers play an especially strong leadership role, do not assign them to cross-affinity teams. However, they may be included on a team "by invitation only" if all members of that team concur. Alternatively, they can be invited by a cross-affinity team to join as a "non-management" participant. This second option works best for managers who are comfortable moving between leadership and participant roles. A third possibility is for the manager to be an observer, leaving

him or her free to wander between teams in order to listen to the discussions from the vantage point of an impartial observer. From time to time, an observing manager might be invited to step into the role of consultant, advising a group on a particular issue, and then move on. Since each option has disadvantages as well as advantages, I usually discuss the range of issues with the management team before the start of the exercise.

Step 3: Charge each team with studying its assigned topic. Team members should develop a clear statement of what the problem is, identify alternatives, and then make a recommendation to the management team. This recommendation is advisory rather than mandatory—managers must still be sold on the idea. However, because delivery of the recommendations will occur during the retrospective, the ideas will be guaranteed a listening audience.

Step 4: Direct each cross-affinity team to its own workspace to begin to dissect the assigned problem. Let people work in groups without interruption for one to two hours. After about two hours, call the groups together and ask them to deliver interim reports. This reporting activity synchronizes the whole community and gives each cross-affinity group a chance to hear comments from other groups before they have formulated a final recommendation.

Step 5: Reassemble everyone. As this exercise takes close to six hours to complete, instruct people to stop discussing issues and break for a meal. Then, after the meal, urge each cross-affinity team to go for a walk as a group. The idea is to give people time to ponder issues without permitting the articulated opinions or arguments of more persuasive group members to interfere. This background processing of all the ideas that have been talked about allows people to assimilate details. Often, at some point during the walk, individual people or entire teams have major breakthroughs about ways to improve the next project.

After the walk, send the cross-affinity teams back to their separate workspaces to continue preparing their problem-analysis statement for management.

Step 6: Pull the teams together to present their completed reports. Make certain that management has an opportunity to respond. If the managers agree to a recommendation, or at least indicate that they would like to pursue an issue further, identify action items, dates for action, and people who will be responsible for the action.

A final note: For some participants, this may be the first time they have been asked to prepare and present a verbal proposal to management, and they may not know the best way to proceed. Novice presenters often state their proposal in the form of "Here is what you need to do." They fail to share the reasoning behind the proposal, behaving as if it were obvious. As facilitator, you may need to help cross-affinity teams articulate their ideas. One way I do this is, during the interim-report break, I ask the managers to describe what they consider to be a good proposal, saying, "What is the best way for these teams to sell an idea to you?" If possible, I also monitor how groups have organized their comments and give what guidance I can throughout the latter parts of Steps 4 and 5. Written directions often help a cross-affinity team get started. A sample of directions I hand out appears later in this section.

Background and theory: The "Cross-Affinity Teams" Exercise is designed to generate the energy and momentum needed to keep key lessons alive long after the retrospective has been concluded. Because the exercise brings a group of diverse people together to talk about what they want to change, the message to management must be viewed as a call to action.

Through the discussion, the community commits to a new way of working, identifying the next steps and making plans to proceed. Expectations are established that next time will be different, and the group understands that it is not just management's responsibility to facilitate the change. As a result, everyone who was involved in the discussion is motivated, and the team becomes empowered.

There is another reason why the exercise is important: The topics that end up on the "What we need to discuss in greater detail" flip chart are often politically loaded issues that spread across affinity groups. They are complex and not well understood, but the exercise fosters discussion among these disparate groups, and encourages people to see a bigger picture.

A True Story

Not long ago, I exchanged e-mail with a colleague who had set up a system for holding retrospectives throughout his company. He had worked for three years to make retrospectives a part of his firm's culture, but the firm had only used a traditional form of retrospective that looked exclusively at the past. The firm did not include planning for the future as part of its retrospective practice. My colleague wrote to me that he had wanted to include a Future component, but the organization's policy limited the time for any one retrospective to half a day.

Before I could suggest any action, he e-mailed again. As it turned out, half-day retrospectives were the good news. The bad news came when, during a reorganization of the firm, directors in the new management decided to study the collection of retrospective reports. They thought the retrospectives would provide good insight into the group's history, as well as suggest steps to take in the future.

However, the new managers soon discovered that the findings from each of the retrospectives for the past three years identified the same problems! Because no improvement occurred over time, they concluded that the retrospectives were ineffective. Their first action was to discontinue retrospectives.

Preparing a Proposal for Management

You have been assigned an important issue that needs to be analyzed so that the next project can experience significant improvement over the one just completed.

The Goal: Develop a proposal for management describing what should change during the next project. You are selling an idea that management may accept, reject, or modify, so promote it as clearly as possible. Some of you may never have tried to sell an idea to management, so you don't know how. If so, as part of this exercise, interview management to learn what it thinks is a good proposal. The following is a template you might use as you assemble your proposal:

Statement of the Problem—Prepare a simple statement outlining the issues to be considered.

Explore the Problem's Impact—Discuss the impact this problem had on the project, citing experiences as evidence. What did the problem cost? (Consider cost from the viewpoint of money, schedule, quality, morale, risk, turnover, health, and market.)

Assess the Risks—Ask your team, "What happens if we do nothing?" If you are suggesting a change, then you need to explain what would happen if no change is made. It is always easiest to not change at all. Explain what might happen during the next project if the status quo is kept. Does this problem get worse? In what ways?

Consider the Future—Ask "Will the next project be different from the previous one?" Is this problem aggravated by differences planned for the next project? Will it have more people? a larger system? a tighter schedule? a new technology?

Options—There must be more than one way to solve your problem. Identify at least three potential solutions. Evaluate the advantages and disadvantages of each.

Recommendation—Recommend one of the alternatives you suggested above and explain why you chose it.

Next Steps—Describe how to put your recommendation into practice, identifying the activities and milestones. If possible, estimate schedule, number of people needed, and size of budget, as well as identify needed policy changes or whatever else is important.

Volunteers—Include in your proposal the names of people on your team who are willing to work with management to help make your recommendation a reality. It is not fair to put the whole burden of initiating change on the shoulders of your management. What are you willing to commit to (if anything)?

Hint: Review the issues, using relevant artifacts and the time line as needed.

In the company described by my True Story e-mail correspondent, canceling retrospectives was exactly the wrong thing to do. Retrospective reports were the best clue these managers had to understanding what was happening in their organization.

The retrospective can help initiate change, but keeping the energy alive is beyond the scope of a retrospective. It is up to the community to continue to work toward a better way of building software. This topic is discussed further in Chapter 10.

THE "MAKING THE MAGIC HAPPEN" EXERCISE

Course: The Future

Purpose: Many times, as I approach the end of a retrospective, I sense that there is one last important topic that has not yet been addressed. The topic varies from group to group, but in all cases it is a topic that proves very difficult to discuss.

When to use: Once, during most retrospectives.

Typical duration: One to two hours.

I use the word "magic" for what happens during this exercise because how it happens is hard to explain. Here is what seems to occur late in the retrospective:

- People are tired and, as a result, most have lowered their guard and are less afraid of voicing their concerns.
- Each person has discovered something about the project that he or she had not realized before.
- People share a collective knowledge about the project, and know more about what went right and what went wrong than at any previous time.
- People who have been taking small risks and are close to saying what needs to be said see that the retrospective provides a safer setting to speak out than in their normal work environment. They feel more open to participating in candid discussions.

- Team members who have been hoping that a certain topic would be raised, now realize the retrospective is nearly at an end, and know that if they don't bring up the issue themselves, it might not be discussed.

All the group needs now is an invitation from you, as the facilitator, to bring up that one last topic. If the topic can be raised successfully, participants usually find this exercise to be one of the most energizing events of a retrospective.

Procedure: This exercise is designed to initiate discussion of a difficult topic in a gentle, careful, and firm manner.

All preceding discussions have led up to this moment. As the facilitator, you will have seen and heard clues about topics that are important but which have not been discussed. The clues will have presented themselves during your interactions with the group, your early discussions with the managers, the pre-work dialogues, the one-on-one discussions you had before the review, and from comments made throughout the retrospective.

Following are typical comments that I have heard over the years:

- "There was too much work. We thought we were supposed to work long hours because everyone else did. The manager matched everyone else's level because he wanted to be with us."
- "Specifications changed continuously. These changes caused the developers to waste a great deal of effort. The community was working in circles, rushing through the specification stage so it would have time to repair the damage done because it had rushed through the specification stage!"
- "The next project might be much bigger than the last one. We feared that what worked before would not scale up."
- "One person did all the organizational chores and tied together loose ends. Because the whole team depended on her, everyone felt vulnerable. If that critical person left, we feared the group would cease to produce software because the remaining staff didn't really possess the knowledge to carry on her work. The critical person was also unhappy—she felt trapped and thought she had been passed over for promotion because she was too valuable in her current role."
- "The manager misunderstood too many communication issues and then acted on his misperceptions. We spent a great deal of time putting out fires that the manager created."

- "Senior engineers continually fought over minute technical issues that didn't really matter to the project. We are tired of the turf battles and mental jousting."
- "Too many managers were directing too few software developers. The result was a highly political multilevel management fight over scarce and worn-out developer resources."

As facilitator, you need to invite that final discussion and then sit back and wait for people to begin speaking from their hearts. There are several ways to get this conversation started:

- Invite the group to speak out by saying, "We are coming to the close of this review. This is a good time to bring up anything that you were hoping we would get to but haven't."
- Reference what people have said by stating, "Throughout this retrospective, I've been hearing about how much effort you gave to make this system a reality. I know that three members of your team could not be here because of this. Take a few moments to reflect on what you personally sacrificed and write it down."
- Speak the unspeakable. First, define the four freedoms as detailed in Chapter 9. Then, in a forthright manner, say, "We have spent days talking about everything except one really important issue. We have worked hard at avoiding the last thing that needs to be said. I want to talk about that." Then let silence do its job. It may be awhile before someone gets the nerve to say something. Once the ice has been broken and the topic broached, group members have at least three options for responding: They can discuss the issue, they can discuss the reasons for not being able to discuss the issue, or they can bring up something completely irrelevant. You can work with the first two options. For the third, record what the person says, then ask, "And what else?"

- Adapt ideas from the "Art Gallery" Exercise described in Chapter 8. I usually use this exercise to help teams with failed projects begin to talk about their experience, but it is also useful to help get the last topic introduced. The "Art Gallery" Exercise lets team members use the right side of their brains to represent the project in pictorial form.

Once the last important issue has been brought up, I record the topic and ask others whether they see it the same way. I encourage more comments and then ask whether someone still sees the issue from a different perspective. If a person speaks in general terms, I ask for specific examples. If someone talks about one particular incident, I inquire, "How often did this happen?" I try to get a realistic perspective on the topic.

Next, I challenge group members to find common ground on the issue, asking them to determine what they all can agree on and what needs to be regarded simply as representing different viewpoints. I want to hear from each of the natural-affinity groups on this topic.

When the community begins to discuss a difficult issue, the facilitator needs to anticipate what will happen and to plan for it. To prepare, try the following:

- Watch the process and guide it. Provide opportunities for everyone to be heard. Demonstrate respect for everyone's opinions as well as their privacy.
- Be willing to work with emotions as they come up. Moist eyes and even tears may appear during this exercise, but this is not a bad sign. Encourage the natural expression of emotions but stay focused on the topic.

To make the magic happen, keep in mind that every group needs something different. I have learned that I must be able to respond immediately and spontaneously to group behavior. I must put my own biases on hold and go with the discussion. As the facilitator, you will need to use your creativity, your experience, and your skills.

The "Change the Paper" Exercise

Course: The Future

Purpose: This exercise ensures that the key findings of the retrospective don't get filed and forgotten.

When to use: Late in the retrospective, usually as one of the final exercises. I use it in most retrospectives. I skip it if I know the team will keep the retrospective lessons alive.

Typical duration: One to two hours.

Background and theory: As stated earlier, the lessons learned from a project retrospective and the ideas of what to do differently next time can be easily forgotten. One way to preserve important details is the old-fashioned way—on paper! Paper can play a pivotal role in keeping issues at the fore as people implement change. Throughout modern history, leaflets, pamphlets, and newsletters have been fundamental to every significant change movement. Conversely, paper can be used to prevent change and to maintain the *status quo* when written rules and guidelines make positive action impossible. I recall many times during my days in academia when various departmental secretaries and even registrars at my university pulled out books on policy to show me—in black and white—why I couldn't take certain classes, couldn't get access to a computer, couldn't be reimbursed, or wouldn't receive course credit.

The "Change the Paper" Exercise is designed to keep the community's memories and interest alive long after the retrospective has ended. The exercise causes team members to look at the role that paper plays in their workplace and helps them change that role, based on the lessons learned in the retrospective. Furthermore, while change is often resisted in a workplace, the medium of paper is rarely protected. Paper is easy to change, with little resistance ever offered.

Procedure: It is probable that as you prepare to facilitate your first few retrospectives, you will review numerous written documents. In addition to the documents, artifacts collected by the community will be made from paper or are information-based and were written on paper. It is a fact that paper plays a key role in most software projects. Some documents are produced and never used, while other documents are used extensively. By taking note of the documents that project members used, you will be helping them take an important step toward defining the software process.

Some of the most important pieces of paper won't be found in a team's files or notebooks but are those tacked to bulletin boards or taped to conference-room walls. Sometimes, they are even found outside the team's work area. Look for them everywhere when you visit the team's workplace.

For this exercise, I usually try one of three different options. Depending on available time and the level of the participants' energy, I may even use more than one in a single retrospective. Following are the three I typically use:

Procedure Option 1 (for teams using complex software development specifications)

Step 1: Introduce the idea that paper is still very important to the way we work despite the increasing utility of the Web. Ask the natural-affinity groups to identify documents they use, such as guidelines, checklists, methodology books, project management templates, process flow maps, defects tracking sheets, work assignments, configuration management reports, status reports, posters, Dilbert cartoons, quick sketches, and even notes scribbled on napkins. Next, stress that you're looking for quality, not quantity—that is, for just the very important documents. If people tell you, "There are none," then that fact is useful, too.

Step 2: Ask the teams to identify which documents need to be changed, given the lessons learned in the retrospective.

Step 3: Ask people to note the changes, develop the plans, and identify anyone who can ensure that the changes are made. Request dates, if practical.

Procedure Option 2 (for teams with writing as a key strength)

Step 1: As above, introduce the importance of paper. Ask team members to describe newsletters and similar publications generated or used regularly within their community.

Step 2: Pursue an opportunity for a pamphlet, a Website, or a news article. If it makes sense to launch a series of articles on lessons from the retrospective to change the way things are done, brainstorm the topics that might go into the essays. See whether there are people interested in writing individual essays or whether someone is interested in pulling the whole series together.

Procedure Option 3 (for teams that use very few documents)
	Step 1: As above, introduce the importance of paper. Note the role of posters in supporting a change to a culture. Try an introduction like this: "During World War II, posters were used to focus an entire country's attention on national security and patriotism. The posters boasted catchy slogans such as 'Loose Lips Sink Ships' and 'Uncle Sam Needs You!' Rosie the Riveter became one of the most famous images from that time. Where have you seen posters used effectively to communicate a goal?" Or, start the exercise with, "Tell me about roadside advertisements that have made an impression on you." Discuss any influence that posters and snappy slogans have had on individual team members' thinking.

	Step 2: Ask people to work in teams to create posters that will reinforce and remind everyone of the lessons learned from this retrospective.

	Step 3: Display the posters and ask the community to discuss them.

	Step 4: Make arrangements to have the posters framed so they can be used as wall hangings, and get the community to discuss where they should be hung. The framed posters will help people remember the messages of the retrospective whenever they see the posters.

A True Story

One team I worked with seemed unable to finish any project before it was canceled. Because the "reset" button had been hit so many times, much of the discussion during the retrospective focused on what these team members needed to stop doing and what they needed to do differently next time. Changes needed to be made at all levels—project management, project design, team organization, scheduling, and so on.

At my suggestion, they created a poster entitled "Don't Do Again." Here is what was listed on it.

Don't Do Again

- Don't build a system the size of an elephant.
- Don't divide the team into subgroups without a means for dialogue between them.
- Don't accept inflexible schedules with conflicting priorities.
- Don't code when we don't know what to build.
- Don't use arbitrary dates as goals.
- Don't plan for mass rollout.
- Don't accept functionality requests from users without authorization from managers.
- Don't trust that people with critical knowledge won't leave the project before they have documented what they know.

I then had them design a second poster entitled "Do Differently This Time." For every item on the first poster, they needed to list at least one item on the second poster indicating what they should do instead.

Do Differently This Time

- Do build a mosquito—very small, very effective, very noticeable, with a short life.
- Do become one group with one focus, one stream of work, one common goal.
- Do deliver a mosquito-sized version of the requested system in a fraction of the time requested.
- Do deliver more functionality in Phases II and III, driven by user feedback.
- Do become masters of analysis and design techniques.
- Do develop our own schedules and set our own goals.
- Do use a small, well-chosen partner/user for our initial rollout.
- Do stop the project if we can't get ample and frequent access to users.
- Do ensure that documents are part of deliverables at each milestone; use peer reviews to ensure that documentation is done.

Team members decided to place these posters in their conference room. Throughout their next project, they turned to the lists to see how they were doing. While working on any given task, if someone saw the project heading back to the old way, he or she could stop the activity and call for a discussion of the activities in the context of the two lists. By pointing out why it seemed the team was headed back to the "Don't Do Again" list, and by checking the work against the "Do Differently This Time" list, the team could change its direction before it was too late.

Doing it "differently this time," the team succeeded—it delivered the system version. But just as important, people on the team discovered that they could control the way they built software. They defined it, and they could change it. As a result of their achievement, they made development of a pair of posters a habit and a goal for each subsequent retrospective. By using retrospectives to define the improvements for the next project, the team could embrace change as a habit and an expectation.

. . . But the story does not end there—during a recent visit to the team's site, I noticed that the first pair of posters was still on the wall. Alongside that first pair were several other pairs. I commented on the lists and one developer explained, "When new people join our team, they are told the history of our group, including what it was like to fail time after time. They are shown our posters, and we explain how we make sure we succeed. It's a powerful and quick way to show how our group has agreed to work, and why. I tell them 'Forget the corporate software development guidelines. These posters document our real software process.'"

References for Further Reading

Bandler, Richard, and John Grinder. *Frogs into Princes: Neuro-Linguistic Programming.* Moab, Utah: Real People Press, 1979 (pp. 79–136).

Anchoring, a very powerful tool used in personal therapy settings to help set and reinforce an intended and desired change, is discussed in depth. By using the activity of reworking paper and, in particular, making posters, I've adapted the concept of anchoring to bring about change in the workplace.

THE "CLOSING THE RETROSPECTIVE" EXERCISE

Course: The Future

Purpose: Every pageant needs to have an ending, and retrospectives are no different. This exercise brings a sense of completion to the work of the project.

Frequency of use: Once, at each retrospective's end.

Typical duration: 10 to 30 minutes.

Procedure: The goal of this final exercise is to shift the community's focus from the work of the retrospective to the real world. The procedure I use to do this generally is derived from some thing that happened during the retrospective. I watch for some theme or incident that can serve as a metaphor for the whole project and then use this topic or episode to create an ending exercise. If nothing suggests itself to you when you are facilitator, you can use the steps below.

> *Step 1: Pass out index cards and pens.* Ask people to write about one hope or wish they have for what will happen after the retrospective, telling them, "Write down something you might care to share anonymously with the community."

> *Step 2: Assemble the cards.* When most people have finished writing, tell them, "When you are done, place your index card writing-side-down in the middle of the floor."

Step 3: Shuffle the cards around on the floor to mix them up.
Ask each person to pick up one card. Give everyone a
turn to read the selected card out loud to the community. After a card has been read, it should be placed
back on the floor, this time writing-side-up.

Step 4: After all the cards have been read, sum things up.
Say something mystical but upbeat, such as, "I see the
possibility of a number of these futures coming to pass.
Now, it's up to you. Make it happen!"

Step 5: Prepare people to return to their jobs, families, and friends. Acknowledge the hard work that has been done. Share any observations or appreciations you have, and then mention that there is a world beyond this room. Talk briefly about moving back into that world. If you used the "I'm Too Busy" Exercise before beginning the actual work of the retrospective, you should still have the collection of "to do" lists people wrote on index cards. Ask whether anyone wants his or her list back. Finally, announce, "This retrospective is officially over."

DESIGNING A RETROSPECTIVE MEAL

In this chapter, I have compared a retrospective to the courses of a meal, and I have presented the dishes for each course in the form of exercises for you to consider as you design your own retrospective meal. Before we move on, let's take a look at the following two pages, which display a sample plan as well as the actual schedule for a retrospective designed by my colleague Diana Larson, and then let's briefly contrast it with the meal I outlined in Chapter 2.

Diana Larson is one of the best general facilitators I've ever met but she had never even heard of a software project retrospective before working with me as I drafted an early version of this book. I asked Diana to lead the retrospective for a project that I had participated in. The project was chartered to build an intranet-based, distributed, *n*-tier sales support application to be deployed globally. In addition to myself, the team consisted of fifteen people from five natural-affinity groups. One customer attended, along with a representative from a third-party software supplier. The project spanned a six-month period. Diana's plan for the retrospective appears as the leftmost column in the tables. What actually occurred can be seen at the right. My observations in italics annotate both columns.

Day One, Planned	Day One, Actual

Day One, Planned

8:30 - 9:00 Introduction
Introduce yourself and answer the questions: Who is one person you admire? Why?

9:00 - 9:45 Discuss Goals
Tell the retrospective's purpose: Tell stories, capture collective wisdom, repair damage to team, enjoy accomplishment.

9:45 - 10:15 Define Success

10:15 - 10:30 Break

10:30 - 11:30 Create Safety
• secret ballot
• ground rules
• second vote

11:30 - 12:00 Artifacts Contest
• most artifacts *(win chocolate)*
• most unusual *(win smoked salmon)*
• most significant *(win great wine)*

12:00 - 1:00 Free Lunch

1:00 - 2:00 Develop the Time Line
Use natural-affinity groups, 5" x 8" cards, different color pen for each group
• cards for join & leave group.
• significant events or happenings
• place card on time line by quarter: summer, fall, winter

2:00 - 4:00 Mine the Time Line
• what worked well?
• lessons learned?
• what to do differently next time?
• what still puzzles us?
• topics needing further discussion

Day One, Actual

8:45 - 9:00 Introduction
Diana asked for intro. to self, for role on project, and for person admired.

9:00 - 9:15 Skipped Goals Discussion
Plan seemed irrelevant. Instead, discussed the schedule and made sure parents with kids would be able to get to child-care in time.

9:15 - 9:55 Define Success

9:55 - 10:10 Break

10:10 - 11:30 Create Safety
Executed as planned.

11:30 - 12:15 Artifacts Contest
Executed as planned.

12:15 - 1:00 Working Lunch
The team listened while the customer said everything she had always wanted to say to those faceless developers back in the home office. *Diana caught the key points on a flip-chart page.*

1:00 - 2:15 Develop the Time Line
• placed cards on time line by months June to January.
• presented effort data as part of the time-line building activity

2:15 - 4:15 Mine the Time Line
Did execute as planned but took ten-minute break at about 3:00.

Day Two, Planned

8:30 - 10:15 <u>Mine Time Line</u>
Continue from yesterday.

Day Two, Actual

8:30 - 10:30 <u>Mine Time Line</u>
We could have used more time mining, but Diana realized we needed to get to the Cross-Affinity Teams group exercise. She kept the pace moving.

10:15 - 10:30 <u>Break</u>

10:30 - 12:00 <u>Mine Time Line</u>
Continue.

10:30 - 10:45 <u>Break</u>

10:45 - 12:00 <u>Begin the Cross-Affinity Teams Exercise</u>
Tried to clarify and prioritize the issues. Discussed cross-team distribution.

12:00 - 1:00 <u>Free Lunch</u>

12:00 - 1:30 <u>Lunch and a Walk</u>
People were getting VERY tired—they needed a change of pace.

1:00 - 3:30 <u>Cross-Affinity Teams</u>
• interim update
• final report

1:30 - 2:00 <u>Cross-Affinity Teams</u>
Worked on issues.

<u>Optional</u>: Review effort measures, personal sacrifices (If they had to do it over again what would they not sacrifice again?), return to the definition of success.

2:00 - 3:00
Tried to facilitate a "quick" update on Cross-Affinity Teams' work. *It took an hour.*

<u>Optional</u>: Offer Appreciations

3:00 - 3:30
Teams developed reports for management.

3:30 - 4:30 <u>Close</u>
Talk about Hopes and Wishes.

3:30 - 3:45
Discussed report findings.

3:45 - 4:00
Discussed how to keep lessons alive. *To "Change the Paper," the entire community designed the wall hangings.*

4:00 - 4:30
<u>Close</u>. Express Prouds and Sorrys. *Diana set the tone by saying, "Think of one thing you are proud of, or sorry about, from the retrospective, that you want to share. Speak as your spirit moves you."*

167

This retrospective, as planned, took two days only. We agreed to the two days because a number of personal schedule conflicts made a three-day event impossible. This book, however, recommends that all retrospectives take three days, plus or minus a half day if circumstances require the modification. So, was the shorter retrospective successful? My answer is, it was not. After attending the two-day event and comparing it to all the three-day reviews I've conducted, I'm convinced that a two-day event cannot adequately address all of the important issues.

Since then, I have determined not to yield to scheduling pressure. It is better to lead a three-day event and deal with a few people coming late or leaving early than to accommodate an event that cannot succeed.

References for Further Reading

Collier, Bonnie, Tom DeMarco, and Peter Fearey. "A Defined Process for Project Postmortem Review," *IEEE Software*, July 1996 (pp. 65–71).

> In their article, the authors define a process and a community a bit different from the ones I write about. I urge you to read the article in order to appreciate another perspective on retrospectives—one in which the technical and managerial leaders are empowered, but possibly at the expense of big-picture learning for the entire community. I would expect their approach to become more attractive as community size increases to a size such as the one they describe of 150 people. The method I describe in *Project Retrospectives* has never been used on a community that large, and I doubt that it would succeed.

A True Story

Many years ago when Tom DeMarco was becoming increasingly well-known as author of the now classic book *Structured Analysis* and *System Specification,* he visited the research lab where I worked. He wanted to see the CASE tools we had developed to support the graphical modeling techniques popularized through his writings. With a great deal of trepidation, I explained to Tom that we had extended his techniques to cover situations that were unique to our user base. I expected to be told that I didn't understand the deep philosophy behind the work and to see all that we had accomplished dismissed as nonstandard. Instead, Tom replied, "I'd much rather have you adapt my work than adopt it. It shows that you are using your brains and are accepting responsibility for your results."

My goal in presenting the methods and exercises in this book is similar to Tom's. Please feel free to adapt rather than adopt. In addition, avoid debates about whose approach is better. Instead, sample the Collier, DeMarco, and Fearey version of retrospectives as well as trying the methods discussed here. By experiencing both approaches and adding a bit of your own creativity, you will find a retrospective style that best fits your organization and uses wisdom from a number of sources.

CHAPTER SEVEN

Leading a Postmortem

Perched high atop a tree late one night, Owl watched as Singed-Tail returned home from a hunting expedition. Rather than announcing his return with his usual barrage of howls and yelps, the wolf crept furtively into his den with the stealth of a hunter trying to escape the notice of his intended prey.

More curious than ever, Owl could barely contain himself until the next morning when he knocked on Singed-Tail's door. His knock was greeted with a growled response, "Get outta here. I ain't seein' nobody."

"It's Owl. I just wanted to hear how your hunt went."

The wolf barked, "Went fine. Just don't wanna talk about it."

Owl pushed for Singed-Tail's reason, "Why's that?"

"Look, maybe we'll talk sometime—say, after my next hunt."

"That's okay." Owl dropped his voice, "I was a bit worried. As you came back last night, I noticed two yellow stripes running down your back. It looked like you might have been run over by a highway road-crew truck."

Bursting from his den, Singed-Tail bared his teeth, "Owl, you better keep your beak closed!"

"Don't worry, my friend. I'm not here to embarrass you. I just thought you might like to talk about what happened. You might discover something to do differently next time."

"I don't need your help! I can think things through on my own. Besides, I'm tired of hunting those three pigs; I'm gonna turn vegetarian!"

No doubt the three pigs had bested Singed-Tail yet again. What Owl had observed late the previous night was a humiliated wolf as he returned home from yet another failure. Singed-Tail's emotions the day after this failure resemble the emotions felt by many project members after a project fiasco. Singed-Tail was *embarrassed*. He *denied* that there were any problems. He wanted to *bargain* for more time before discussing hunting. He was *angry* and became *threatening*. He was *discouraged* and even *depressed*—so much so that he vowed to stop eating meat. His confidence about his ability to be a big, bad wolf had hit rock bottom.

Overwhelmed by these emotions, the wolf felt too much pain to think about the hunt. Owl, however, knew that it was this very pain that could provide the motivation for Singed-Tail to actually learn better ways to hunt—but he would need to actively review his experience.

It is my conviction that there is no better way to recover from a *failed* project than to participate in an effective retrospective, one that is truly a *project postmortem*. In this chapter on failed projects, I deliberately use the word *postmortem* rather than *retrospective*. "After death" seems to be the best way to describe a review of the kinds of projects I discuss here—projects that failed, and failed seriously! Failed—as in, $3 million has been spent and there is nothing to show for it and there is no projected date indicating when the system might work. Failed—as in, if the system were used, it could kill people, damage property, or cause the loss of vast amounts of money!

The postmortem provides an invaluable learning experience precisely because a failed project contains many important clues about what needs changing. With clear evidence that the project failed, these clues cannot be ignored. An honest, soul-searching assessment is more likely to result from the postmortem of a failed project than will be revealed through review of a partially successful project. With the latter, people tend to rationalize, "After all, we did deliver something."

We have dramatic failures such as are described above—in fact, they are all-too common in our business—but not much is written about them, except for the occasional Monday-morning-quarterback analysis performed by an outsider whose purpose is to find fault. It is rare for a team to look carefully and methodically at its own failure to see what can be learned, yet this is exactly what needs to happen. A major project failure doesn't happen because of one or two wrong decisions, nor is it the fault of one or two people. Big projects fail when *all* of the following conditions are true:

- Important decisions were made poorly or were not made at all.

- Safeguards that should reveal problems early did not exist or did not work.

- Team members either could not or would not speak up to say that the project was in trouble, or if they did say something, their words were not heeded.

All people-based systems—such as management, engineering, quality assurance, process development, risk analysis, funding, communication, and community protocol systems—and all hiring, firing, and advancement policies contribute in some part to big-project failure. Analysis of failure can initiate significant positive change throughout a firm, extending well beyond the group that experienced the failure. Although the failure may have occurred within only one group, the entire organization's culture is likely to have contributed to the failure in some way. Therefore, diagnosis of a failure requires a careful and fearless analysis of the entire organization to see what needs to be reengineered.

The best time to review all software development practices is when the memory of the failure is freshest. There are likely to be other potential failures waiting to occur. Why then are so few postmortems held? The following story illustrates the dichotomy between what we think should be and what is.

The Challenger Story

While preparing to facilitate my first large postmortem in 1988, I wondered what best to model failure analysis on so as to make the benefits unequivocal. Researching the topic, I found that a great deal had been written about why businesses or marriages fail, but I wanted an example more applicable to my client's project, one that would illustrate analyzing failure and growing beyond it. I came across one subject index that cited project-failure analysis in terms of the January 1986 explosion of the Space Shuttle *Challenger*. The events leading up to the tragedy struck me as important to study. I knew that the National Aeronautics and Space Administration had grounded all space launches immediately following the disaster, devoting the ensuing months to reengineering each process and procedure used prior to the accident, and to reexamining all its policies and practices.

Hoping to find more information, I headed to the nearest bookstore to research how NASA learned from and coped with the failure. What I found astonished me—although there were a vast number of government and scientific documents written on the *Challenger* explosion, only five mass-market books were listed on the subject. Four of the books were written for school-children to help them cope with the fact that a young teacher had died in the accident. Only one of the listed books targeted the adult market—*Challenger: The Final Voyage* by Richard S. Lewis—and it was not in stock.

The lack of literature confirmed my belief that people are reluctant to study failure! Self-examination is hard, but I believe we can learn *more* from studying our failures than from our successes. With our failures, we know something went wrong. With our successes, we wonder how much of what we did was pure chance.

Our culture has taught us about succeeding and winning, but we don't learn how to lose in a healthy way. From Pee Wee League teams to high-school intramurals to the Olympics, we learn that we are to "bring home the gold." If we don't, we feel shame and disappointment. Our culture conditions us to feel this way, but the feeling is only one of many possible reactions. Another way to react is to embrace the failure as an opportunity to learn, saying, "Now I know for sure that I have something to learn."

TRANSFORMING THE FAILED-PROJECT EXPERIENCE

The phrase "use of self" is common in the facilitation field but it puzzled me when I was first learning to facilitate and consult. I came to understand that it means using my presence, my actions, my comments, and my responses to elicit healing behavior among people in the community. Because they

look to me for guidance, I can affect the attitudes of people with the way I respond and lead.

One key idea the facilitator must convey is that failure is just one possible outcome. The experience of failure is okay to talk about and learn from. It should not carry shame or guilt or blame. It is an experience that should awaken curiosity and a passion to improve. Your goal as facilitator is to establish in the community a sense of pride in the wisdom acquired by a fearless and meticulous review, and a commitment to change.

Leading a truly effective postmortem may very well be the most satisfying work a facilitator can do. Within the span of a few days, a disappointed, fragmented group of people can be transformed into a team with a clear focus and a desire to proceed. Managers who ask for a postmortem usually are people who value learning how to improve more than they fear the repercussions of failure. They are true leaders, worthy of their team's trust and the responsibility their firm has given them.

As facilitator, you occupy an important position. You may be the first person outside the team to view the entire project. In one sense, you are an authority figure. How much the community accepts you and lets you see depends entirely on you. To help people accept you fully, you need to communicate the attitude that the project is only a failure if the community does not learn from it. Show that you honestly believe that each member of the community did the best he or she could, given what was known at the time. Convey your conviction that by working with team members, you and they will figure out what to do differently next time. Demonstrate that you are capable of discretion and of honest communication, making it safe for the community to share its secrets. See that everyone understands that you are not there to pass judgment, but only to guide community members as they discover what they need to learn. Be a good listener as you help people create an environment within which the project can be explored safely.

Consultants who confuse their customary role of giving advice with their current role of being neutral postmortem facilitators can do irreversible harm by imposing their opinions. When a facilitator ceases to be neutral, participants may feel unsafe and communication will stop. No matter how much you want to give the community answers or seize a teachable moment, *don't do it.* Instead, use your experience and your insight to gently lead community members into finding their own answers.

When preparing for a postmortem, assess the community's mood and current state of mind. Determine whether people have adopted a coping strategy that will prevent a successful postmortem from occurring. When I observe teams that have experienced a recent project failure, I usually see at least one of

177

the following three coping behaviors. These behaviors, which are common among people who feel they have failed, are

- saving face
- grieving over loss
- accepting a lowered self-esteem

Saving Face

A person's sense of failure may be so great that he or she will feel unable to bear it. One approach people typically use to cope with their sense of failure is called "saving face." Saving face entails an attempt to preserve dignity in spite of the situation and is an almost instinctive approach people use to avoid feelings of failure. There are numerous face-saving stances but most involve accepting a bit of fantasy as reality. Often, the fantasy makes little sense to an impartial observer while it is clearly believable to those involved. Following are some of the face-saving fantasies that people may adopt:

- *Declare the project a success:* The team declares the project a success and ensures that no one asks too many questions. There is usually a shroud of secrecy around the project and facts are difficult to determine. Key people on the project might whisper bits of the story, but soon the corporate memory forgets the failed aspects of the project and the manufactured truth gets retold and embellished.
- *Establish blame elsewhere:* Group members find one individual or perhaps even a few people to blame for the failure. This is odious behavior as the "guilty" party might lose his or her job, or be stripped of responsibilities. Along with their mission to establish who is to blame, people who seek retribution probably harbor a great deal of anger. The truth is that many people feel guilty over the failure of a project, and may move as fast as they can to blame someone else. Of course, the

scapegoat is rarely the person who created the problems, but often is the one who put the most effort into trying to solve them.

- *Subordinate the project to something "more important:"* The group shifts priorities and suggests that the project can "go on the shelf for a while." People who try this approach contend that the market has shifted, or the customer base has shifted, or other opportunities are now more important, and that, as a result, they need to stop the current effort.

- *Purchase a silver-bullet remedy:* Team members believe they can find a third-party supplier of a system that will be better and cheaper than the one that has failed. The reality is that this off-the-shelf purchase probably will be less functional than the failed system, or that such a system does not even exist as a product for purchase.

- *Claim that the job simply couldn't be done:* Project team members accept that it was an aggressive project, which was good for them to attempt at the time, but which was loaded with risk. They rationalize that, given those circumstances, they couldn't have been expected to complete it. While this may sound healthy, watch for the next phrase: "Since we couldn't do it, that proves that it couldn't be done." This means that people have accepted that failure was the only possible outcome.

- *Hide project demise:* During a down-sizing activity, many projects are reduced or canceled as a result of a "difficult but fiscally responsible act on senior management's part." The fault is placed not on the project but on economic hard times. The typical scramble that follows, as management looks for projects that can absorb displaced workers, assures that no one asks too many questions about any of the canceled projects.

Even though they are dysfunctional, these face-saving tactics are a natural way for people to rationalize that a failure was a success. As facilitator, you need to understand the state of mind of your postmortem community and make allowances for it. Schedule postmortem assignments according to the group's frame of mind. Structure your pre-work efforts, early site visits, and selection of exercises to accommodate the community's current needs and to help people take a more realistic view of their failure—use an approach that awakens curiosity and a passion to improve, and that helps them establish pride in their wisdom while building their commitment to change. Remember: Saving face involves maintaining one's dignity. Deploying Kerth's Prime Directive (see Chapter 1) is key to ensuring that people's dignity is protected while they explore their experience.

Grieving Over Loss

To see how this second coping behavior can take form, think back to the fable of Singed-Tail. Not ready to review his misadventure despite Owl's sympathetic encouragement, the wolf reacted by denying his failure, trying to bargain, venting anger, and then by succumbing to a period of depression.

Humans experience these same emotions as the result of a loss. Elisabeth Kübler-Ross, the famous Swiss psychiatrist and noted author of *On Death and Dying*, researched people's reactions to loss, studied in the extreme context of facing their own death or that of someone close. Although the loss of a project undeniably is less devastating than the losses Kübler-Ross studied, the software developer who has made serious sacrifices to create a system "no matter what" will have become very attached to the future outcome. If the project is stopped, the developer's natural reaction can be a grief similar to that associated with death.

The work of Kübler-Ross details five distinct stages that people who are faced with loss move through, sometimes moving sequentially in the order listed here but not always. The stages of denial, anger, bargaining, depression, and acceptance are described below in terms of software projects.

In *denial*, people refuse to believe that the project has failed. In any large community, there will be people who do not believe that the project has really been canceled, who even continue with their work. Others may believe that the project is merely on hold, expecting that it will be restarted in a few weeks. In such cases, my job is to help individuals see reality. After asking them questions about their world view, I use their answers to reveal to them what I observe to be true.

During the *anger* stage, people may exhibit hostility and even rage. They resent the sacrifices they have made, sometimes to the point of irrationality. Although often considered to be destructive, anger can be therapeutic if vented in a healthy manner. From personal experience, I've come across several activities that may mitigate anger—such as writing a no-holds-barred letter (but not sending it), punching a pillow, storming about or yelling in an empty room, or exercising vigorously. Such venting activities lend physical action and voice to counteract emotions stirred up by the anger-causing events that occurred during the project.

During *bargaining*, attempts at negotiation take place. People plead, "What do we need to do differently to keep this project going?" They ask for another chance. When facilitating a project whose members are in this stage, you are likely to receive weak and flawed assessments designed to demonstrate how close the project is to actually being successful. When I meet someone who is in the bargaining stage, I rarely need to do anything. Bargain-seekers usually come to the conclusion that the strategy will not work. However, sometimes I urge them to write down their assessment, recommending that they provide comprehensive, clearly written estimates accompanied by well-documented reasons. In many cases, the act of collecting and organizing the data is enough to help them discover the weaknesses in their arguments and to move them out of the bargaining stage.

People who sink into a project-related, temporary state of *depression* will seem to have totally given up. Typically, they feel defeated. They go through the motions of working but feel

181

as if they have too little energy to be truly productive again. When I see people this disheartened, I acknowledge that what they are feeling makes sense to me, telling them that I have been there, too. I ask questions but I don't give answers. I propose tasks geared to involving them in achievable assignments they can work on throughout the postmortem. I help them begin to think about what would be a good next job—one which they could approach with curiosity and excitement, and one in which they could experience growth and joy.

People in a state of depression may contemplate a career change, but this is usually the wrong time for them to act on their feelings. If you learn that someone is considering a serious change, ask how long he or she has been thinking about it. If it has only been for a short while, urge the individual to take things slowly. When in this state, people rarely make wise decisions.

Acceptance is the stage at which the need for coping ends. Once acceptance of the failed project has occurred, people can get on with their lives and the community and facilitator can get on with learning from the project postmortem.

I use this model of the five stages of coping to help managers understand events in their organization. At the end of a failed project, a firm may choose to break up the team and distribute the people to a number of understaffed projects across the company. Human resource and project managers are likely to make incorrect decisions about what people coming off of a failed project are capable of if they observe people in their coping states. Managers need to understand that these coping stages are not permanent, and that the behavior does not represent what the worker has to offer long-term.

I have watched a number of people whose managers thought of them as poor performers work through the stages of coping during a postmortem and emerge as significant players in the weeks and months to come.

Accepting a Lowered Self-Esteem

Besides exhibiting face-saving and grieving behavior, people whose projects have failed may experience a general loss of self-esteem. Nathaniel Branden, author of *The Six Pillars of Self-Esteem,* identifies five characteristics common to people with healthy levels of self-esteem.

- confidence in one's ability to think
- confidence in one's ability to cope with the basic challenges of life
- confidence in one's right to be successful and happy
- confidence in being worthy, deserving, and entitled to assert one's needs and wants
- confidence in being entitled to achieve one's goals and to enjoy the fruits of one's labor

In his book, Branden describes how a person's level of self-esteem impacts his or her rationality, grasp of reality, intuitiveness, benevolence, creativity, independence, flexibility, ability to manage change, willingness to admit and correct mistakes, and ability to cooperate.

Experiencing a failed project can cause people to doubt the way they think, cope, and assert their rights, making them feel less worthy to express opinions or to provide leadership.

The development of one's healthy self-esteem should be a life-long practice. Whether high or low, the level of your self-esteem is re-set and maintained daily. An event such as a failed project can dramatically affect self-esteem. For most people, a failed project will result in lower self-esteem, but a person who actively works to maintain self-confidence may find that facing a failure head-on helps one move past the failure.

Low self-esteem may be characterized by specific personality traits and moods, such as varying degrees of guardedness, paranoia, intolerance of others' mistakes, stifled creativity, repression, and an inability to take risks. None of these character disorders is conducive to a successful postmortem.

A further problem is that *temporarily* lowered self-esteem, if left unaddressed, can become *habitually* lowered self-esteem. As a facilitator, you have a chance to transform a project team's perspective and help people learn to deal with failure—an accomplishment that can increase their feelings of confidence and worth, making them productive once again.

Branden identifies six pillars upon which a healthy self-esteem can be constructed. Paraphrased, the six pillars are

- *The practice of living consciously:* Become more aware of all that might go on within a project, and do not automatically work as you have in the past simply out of habit.

- *The practice of self-acceptance:* Accept that you are a human with strengths and weaknesses, and believe that you have something significant to contribute to the project.
- *The practice of self-responsibility:* Own the results of your actions and choose to be empowered to effect those results.
- *The practice of self-assertiveness:* Know you have a place on the team and valuable contributions to make.
- *The practice of living purposefully:* Approach your work and your profession with some greater purpose in mind than simply that "It's a job."
- *The practice of personal integrity:* Exercise a moral creed to align how you think, what you say, and how you act, keeping your thoughts consistent with your actions and words.

As you interact with the retrospective's participants, look for signs of people coping with lowered self-esteem. Keep Branden's six pillars in mind and employ them appropriately. Weave them into exercises, into your discussions, and into your facilitation. You may have to be the enforcer to redirect actions counter to each of these pillars, but if so, intervene only from the perspective that coping behavior is natural. It is neither bad nor good, but just the way things are.

Exercises that promote self-esteem are useful. For example, the "Artifacts Contest" Exercise and the "Develop a Time Line" Exercise contribute to living consciously. The rule that states "everything is optional" and the "Create Safety" Exercise support self-responsibility and lead to personal integrity. The establishment of natural-affinity teams or cross-affinity teams encourages self-assertiveness. The "Mining the Time Line for Gold" activity and the "Change the Paper" Exercise further living purposefully.

Qualifying to Lead a Postmortem

Given the complexities of a community coping with a failed project, before you accept the assignment to facilitate, you need to assess whether you are fully qualified to lead the particular postmortem. How can you know? Answering the following questions can help you evaluate your readiness.

First, honestly evaluate how much experience you have had leading people under stress and how good you are at it. Are you comfortable facilitating sessions in which emotions are strong? Are you capable of dealing with a team's negative energy?

If you answer "no," "maybe," "don't know," "not really," or "did it once," *you would be unwise to facilitate by yourself.* Partner with someone who can answer these questions affirmatively and have him or her teach you how to handle complex situations.

Some Important Differences Between Retrospectives and Postmortems

While a retrospective and a postmortem involve the same procedures and share the same goals, there are differences between the two. A postmortem is a more in-depth, intense, and demanding undertaking than a retrospective, leaving little room for a facilitator to take a risk or make a mistake. It needs to be longer than a retrospective, which typically will range from two-and-a-half to three-and-a-half days. A postmortem, on the other hand, should span three-and-a-half to four-and-a-half days. Although I usually recommend that a retrospective be residential, I require that a postmortem be residential because there is so much more to explore, learn, heal, and plan that you need the extra time a residential setting provides.

As you prepare for a postmortem, allocate more time to review pre-work and more time to follow up either by phone or in person than you would normally devote. Even more important for a postmortem than for a retrospective, you will need to contact any people who have left the project. Interview them and, in cases in which their presence would be advantageous, invite them to be part of the postmortem.

Another difference between a retrospective and a postmortem pertains to the number of participants. In a retrospective, I feel comfortable leading about thirty people by myself. In a postmortem, I'll partner with another facilitator whenever the team is larger than fifteen members.

Although the exercises designed for a retrospective work well in a postmortem, I add some additional exercises for a postmortem. Some are pertinent early in the postmortem to address the coping reactions mentioned above, and a few are meant to be used throughout to establish pride of wisdom where there once might have been shame from failure. In the following chapter are specific exercises you might want to include in a postmortem that you will rarely, if ever, need for a retrospective.

CHAPTER EIGHT

Postmortem Exercises

With intermittent flapping of his wings, Owl was hard at work on his Recipes for Life *book when he was interrupted by quite a racket. Offering his usual salutation, "Who? Who?" Owl looked down to see Beaver passing by lugging a most unusual piece of equipment. "Beaver, what is that?"*

"Oh, hello, Owl. This is my Scubamajig," Beaver replied. "I'm working in the Black Lagoon today. You know Scalely, that retired movie star? He wants me to install a private movie theater in his lair. He likes watching his old movies."

Owl hooted, "Yes, I know him, . . . an interesting creature. One of the nicest monsters you will ever meet." Growing more curious, Owl continued, "I've never seen you use that tool before. Is it new?"

"Nope," replied Beaver, "I just use this every once in a while. For some jobs, you just need special tools. You see, Scalely's new movie theater will be under water."

As Beaver clattered away, Owl wrote himself a reminder to decline Scalely's invitation to his Return of the Monsters Film Festival. He then began to think about using special tools for special jobs.

THE EXERCISES

The exercises described in this chapter are designed to handle the various circumstances a facilitator may encounter during a postmortem. What makes the exercises especially suitable for use during a postmortem is that each is designed with the goal of enabling the learning that's possible from failure.

A True Story

Several years ago, my colleague Jean McLendon and I teamed up to lead a postmortem. Emotions were unusually high among team members and their management. Several million dollars had been spent with nothing to show for it, and litigation had begun.

After a long day of one-on-one interviews, Jean and I were still unsure as to why we had been called in, and so the two of us headed off by ourselves to a restaurant to compare notes. It was clear from the one-on-one interviews that project members had thought about the project and could comment on what they would do differently in the future—but there was something odd about what we were hearing. The comments seemed superficial, lessons were not discussed with passion, and no one was using the "f" word. That is, no one seemed to be able to admit that the project was a failure! People knew intellectually that it was a failure, but they couldn't talk about it as such.

Jean and I realized that this community wouldn't learn what needed to be learned until people could talk honestly and openly about what it was like to fail. Somewhere in the community's culture, the discussion of failure was seen as taboo. We needed to change this notion.

Jean suggested that we invite the company's chief executive officer and its vice president of Information Services to come to the first part of the postmortem so that she could interview them in front of their staff about the presence of failure in their lives and careers, and about what the long-term effect had been. The goal was to establish the value and importance of learning from failure. The executives accepted the invitation, settling in easily as Jean guided the interview questions to be certain all members of the community came away understanding the following points:

- The executives recognized that failure does sometimes happen, and that a failure is something from which people can learn.
- Their project had failed—and failed big.
- No one was going to get fired as a result of admitting that the project was a failure.
- The community had better learn how to prevent such a massive failure next time, because the company couldn't afford another of that magnitude!

This interview session successfully broke down the barriers that had been preventing project members from openly discussing the reasons why the project failed. By means of the session, implicit permission was given to people to be honest about the issues.

191

The community was ready to examine its failure, and the remainder of the postmortem was charged with discussion of lessons learned.

There was one particularly interesting outcome of this postmortem meeting. Because members of the community could now talk about failure, they could also talk about success. By the end of the postmortem, participants had identified fifteen tasks or procedures that they had learned to do amazingly well, and that could now be considered assets. Before the postmortem, no one had realized that significant gains had occurred in the department alongside the failures. Jean's idea of interviewing executives about their failures developed into the "CEO/VP Interview" Exercise.

The "CEO/VP Interview" Exercise

Course: The Readying.

Purpose: This exercise is designed to help participants become comfortable with the idea of talking about failure without feeling shame.

When to use: Use this exercise when members of the community have difficulty with the idea that they have failed, as well as whenever you see evidence of the coping tactics discussed in Chapter 7.

Typical duration: 60 minutes.

Procedure: Ask for a list of the firm's leaders—those people highest up in the management chain who have the best reputation, the complete respect of the community, and the confidence to be interviewed about their failures in front of their staff. Although you can make the necessary points with only one role model if no other executive seems right for the task, your goal is to find two candidate executives who are willing to be interviewed.

Meet with the candidates and explain that community members need to see someone they respect model the process of learning from failure. Establish a rapport with the executives so that they trust that you won't embarrass or attack them. The interview is not meant to be an exposé, but rather a dialogue in which empathy and consideration are shown the individual being interviewed. Prior to the interview, ask the executives to outline the stories they want to share, then comment on the stories to give them an indication of the boundaries you'll observe as you interview.

Start the postmortem with this interview exercise. Jump right into it, postponing discussion of procedural items, an agenda, or any of the other issues in the "Introduction" Exercise until later.

To introduce the exercise, summarize the events that led up to the *Challenger* failure, citing the details I noted in Chapter 7. Begin a dialogue by saying, "I think we would all agree that the 1986 *Challenger* Space Shuttle explosion was the result of a failed project. I imagine you would think that many people would have studied the failure and written about it, right? How many books for the general populace would you guess were published within the first few years after the accident?" Field a few guesses and then tell them, "Five—with all but one of those written for children!"

Next, ask, "Why do you think so little was published?" Encourage discussion, and then continue, "I think one reason is because we are uncomfortable talking about failure. How often do you get to talk—honestly and safely—about failure at work before going on to a new project? Is such discussion common? Give me a show of hands if you think it's common here."

Comment on the number of hands raised. If there are few hands, then share the fact that this is the way most firms work. Smile and say, "You are in good company." Point out that failure provides an excellent experience from which to learn. Ask, "Why don't we discuss failure? Is it because we fear that we might be penalized or even fired?" See whether anyone wants to comment, acknowledging that this kind of frank discussion is difficult.

If more than half of the participants raise their hands, compliment the community, letting people know that their ability to discuss failure is impressive, and assure them they are ready to learn from their experience.

To introduce the executive interviews, begin by saying something like, "I'd like to demonstrate that discussing failure is okay, good, and even the right thing to do. I've asked two executives to describe their failures and to tell us what those failures meant to their careers—both short-term and long-term. These people will serve as our role models for open discussion of failure."

Then, begin the interviews. Ask each executive to describe his or her position in the company, number of years with the company, previous positions held, and so on. Next, ask each to describe a significant career failure. Finally, ask the executives to explain what they learned from the failure and how it shaped their career.

At the end of an hour, thank the executives for their openness, and then call for a break. The break provides time during which information can sink into people's minds, and gives individuals a chance to comment informally to each other. After the break, start the "Introduction" Exercise.

THE "ART GALLERY" EXERCISE

Course: Late in the Readying course or early in the Past course.

Purpose: To help people become comfortable discussing their project.

When to use: Use whenever there are no executives available to be interviewed but the community is not describing the experience using the word "failure."

Typical duration: 60 minutes.

Procedure: To start the analysis of the group's failure, I ask natural-affinity teams to find their own space, taking with them a flip-chart pad and colored pens. I tell members of each group to do the "Art Gallery" Exercise by using only the right side of their brains, that is, without talking. My instructions are: "Collaborate to draw one picture of what it was like to be on this project. This is to be a picture derived without any discussion."

As each picture is completed, I ask the artists to discuss their work among themselves and then to add a title to their picture. The next step is to place the pictures side-by-side on a wall and invite the entire community to gather around. The

artists from each natural-affinity team are then asked to describe their works of art. After they have presented their work, I ask other members of the community whether they have any questions. As the discussion continues, a composite picture begins to emerge from which participants can compare the experiences illustrated by the various groups' drawings.

What we are doing in the "Art Gallery" Exercise is beginning to tell the stories of the whole project. The drawings provide a great way to introduce the idea that this project may be seen from many different viewpoints. The session opens up the chance for someone to take a risk anonymously, or to depict some painful aspect of the project, perhaps with a bit of humor.

The drawing session provides a nice way to let people ease into telling their story.

Background and theory: In her breakthrough book, *Drawing on the Right Side of the Brain,* Betty Edwards explores ways to tap underused areas of the brain. The "right side" designates the part of the brain that allows one an awareness of concepts to be sensed without the use of words. This side of the brain does not operate on use of reason or facts, yet it aids us in reading conclusions intuitively. It provides a rich source of creativity.

Edwards explains that we can access this valuable part of our brain through drawing. The results often astound us as we let our left side of the brain analyze and put into words what was produced by our right side.

This exercise begins as a non-talking exercise because we want the right side of the brain, the nonverbal side, to be in control. It is a group activity that uses natural affinity to aid mutual suggestion and thus deeper exploration.

Once the drawing has been produced, the activity of finding a title for each picture invites left-brain analysis through discussion among the collaborators. Words are now used to describe the often surprising pictures, and a new understanding of the project experience can begin.

THE "DEFINE INSANITY" EXERCISE

Course: This exercise may be used late in the Readying course, or during the Past course, especially as a substitute for the "Session Without Managers" Exercise, if such a session is requested as part of the postmortem. I've also used this exercise with a community that was considering a postmortem but which feared that such a session would turn ugly. This exercise is especially effective when used to demonstrate that a blame-free review can be conducted.

Purpose: Some groups have experienced not just one but a series of failures. Most likely, their software process, profes-

197

sional practice, and management style all ensure failure. Individuals in such groups feel like victims trapped in an impossible situation. I use this exercise when I see a series of failed projects with participants who say they feel like victims. For such people, the exercise helps them recognize that they have power and can effect change.

When to use: As needed.

Typical duration: One to two hours.

Procedure: This exercise has several steps.

> *Step 1: Provide a working definition of insanity.* Tell the community that you have your own definition of insanity, and you want to share it. Write the definition on a flip chart:
>
> > *Insanity means doing the same thing you did in the past but expecting different results.*
>
> *Step 2: Ask participants for examples of insanity from their own project experience.* Ask whether anyone has experienced the kind of insanity described in the definition. Then ask for examples of things that people keep doing while expecting new results. List each example on a flip chart. Ask enough questions so that everyone understands what each example is about. You may be able to combine several ideas into a single item on the flip chart, or you might need to break an overly general concept into several smaller, more concise statements. As people exhaust their examples or as you finish off about two pages, close the discussion and title the list "Don't Do Again."
>
> *Step 3: Encourage discussion of alternatives.* Move to a second flip chart and label a clean sheet of paper "Do

Differently Next Time." For each item listing an example of insanity, have the community find a counteraction that it can agree on for next time. Check that each "Do Differently" item is realistic. If not, help people identify a good alternative.

Step 4: Select follow-on exercises to complement the identified goals. Use the results of this exercise to select the contents of the rest of the exercises you run. In the "Develop a Time Line" Exercise, you will be able to skip over some of the obvious lessons learned because they are already on your "Do Differently Next Time" list. In the Future course, you can include these lists as part of the exercises for "Cross-Affinity Teams," "Making the Magic Happen," and "Change the Paper."

A True Story, Revisited

If this exercise sounds a bit familiar, it should. The team members described in the story told in the "Change the Paper" Exercise in Chapter 6 used the results of their discussion to make posters. Recall that that team's members had listed "Don't build a system the size of an elephant" and "Don't use arbitrary dates as goals" as reminders of what not to do next time. However, for that team, finding and listing counteractions seemed impossible as the features required and the time allowed were dictated by upper management. I reminded team members that these lists can be thought of as a "Declaration of Independence from the Past," stating, "Let's write down what we need to do differently next time, and then figure out how we can make such a project happen." After further discussion and brainstorming sessions, they decided on two important actions:

- Do build a mosquito—very small, very effective, very noticeable, with a short life.
- Do develop our own schedules and set our own goals.

With these counteractions noted on the "Do Differently Next Time" flip chart, we set about to see how we might proceed—following the goals set by upper management but working according to the developers' own (sane) terms. Team members decided they could build a *piece* of the required system and deliver it in two or three months, rather than attempt to build the entire system in the dictated (but impossible) nine months.

They prepared a proposal for management, pointing out that after the series of failures, they needed to try something small. The developers stated that they would be in charge of identifying which piece of the overall system they would build, but that it would provide significant utility to their users. By the end of the postmortem, they had developed a convincing plan, which management accepted.

It took team members five months to build the selected system piece, delivering about one third of the entire requested system. Users were now happy and encouraged, excited that an important piece of the desired system was delivered early!

During the five months, a phased approach to software development had become part of the management style, and plans for Phase Two indicated that the team would build the second third of the system within the next three months. Efficiency was up, process mastery was up, morale was up, and user confidence was up.

Because of the success of Phase One, and because high-level management had confidence that Phase Two would be delivered ahead of the original nine-month schedule, no one truly cared that the unrealistic, dictated schedule was being ignored. Instead, team members were left to build incrementally and upper management focused on exploring the candidate features of Phase Three and procuring third-phase funding.

Four months after the completion of Phase Three, promotions and company-wide recognition were given to those who "built a mosquito when the users asked for an elephant, and figured out how to build it smaller and faster than requested."

Theory and background: By providing a definition of insanity, and then by asking the community to give examples of insanity using that definition, a facilitator can promote a safe discussion of software process flaws without the conversation degenerating into an attack on any one person. If it is clear that the discussion is not about individuals, it easily becomes an analysis of the software development process. In cases in which participants seem resistant, assure them that, since the team as a whole has had a series of failures, it is certain that the problem is the group's way of working, not the fault of particular individuals.

The first step, asking team members about their particular insanity, helps focus the discussion on what has been going on and what habits are problematical. The second step, labeling the insanity as "Don't Do Again," is a subtle step toward causing the community to change. The community has agreed that these practices are insane. The act of labeling the list serves the purpose of defining and naming the goal in a way that no one can argue against. In *Influence,* a book on marketing trends and methods, Robert Cialdini calls this persuasive effect *social proof*—that is, a group will follow social norms if they are norms the group has established.

The third step generates the "Do Differently Next Time" statements and allows empowerment to occur. The community gets to dream of an alternative way of working that avoids the insanity. This new vision then feeds the Future course activities. The "Do Differently Next Time" list breaks a difficult task into manageable pieces. It also serves as a reminder and an anchor back to the moment when the community decided to stop the insanity.

THE "MAKE IT A MISSION" EXERCISE

Course: The Future.

Purpose: This exercise is intended to transform a failed experience into a mission to change the firm's software development process, to establish pride in the ability to learn from mistakes, and to help all members of the community become experts on how the firm's common software development process must change.

When to use: Select this exercise when discoveries found during the postmortem have widespread implications for the firm.

Typical duration: Two to four hours.

Procedure: Simply stated, a postmortem could be used to launch a revolution. It can excite project members so much about what they learn that they want to carry their message throughout their organization. Passion and purpose to change the company can easily grow out of a team's analysis of failure. As a facilitator, you may have to help team members translate this dream into reality.

In this "Make It a Mission" Exercise, you are teaching people how to become activists—how to work to change a community. Because this topic is too complex to cover completely in this handbook, I refer you to the works of Judith L. Boice and Saul D. Alinsky for additional information (see the reference section at the end of this exercise). I can, however, make some suggestions here for you to convey to your community:

- *Have a clear mission.* Establish agreement about your overall goal by developing a mission statement.
- *Remove ego from the message.* Present the message because it is the right thing to do, not because it is good for your career.
- *Cultivate vision, persistence, confidence, and optimism.* Demonstrate each of these characteristics as you begin to take the message to the rest of the organization. Make it a regular practice to measure how well you are doing in each of these four areas.
- *Plan to educate, and present your message often.* Adults can learn, but most need to hear the message many times in many different ways. They need to reflect on the message as they consider their own experiences.

- *Invite others in the company to join you.* A grass-roots movement is more likely to succeed if many people join in and deliver the message of change.
- *Create a newsletter.* Every active change movement needs a way to communicate—a clearing house through which announcements can be made, to encourage continuation of the learning and thinking process, and to focus a community. A print or electronic newsletter is just such a clearing house. Whether it arrives directly in the hands or on the screen, either type is preferable to a Website, which is passive and only works if people actually visit the site.

- *Be inclusive of others' ideas.* Many activist efforts fail because of infighting. From the start, show by your inclusive attitude that all ideas are welcome and a difference of opinion is okay, as long as everyone is working to accomplish the mission statement.
- *Be a respectful change agent, rather than a zealot.* Discuss the issues, listen closely in order to understand others' opinions, search for common ground, and adopt a position that fits both parties' ideas—or, agree to disagree.
- *Live your own message.* No matter what changes you may or may not effect throughout the company, use what you have learned to modify how you work.

Change-effecting activities for team members to explore as part of planning their mission might include

- making a presentation to top-level management on ways to prevent future failures
- developing a presentation to be given to the entire firm
- writing a regular column in the company newsletter
- creating a company-wide committee to address change in the software process
- establishing a long-term company-wide initiative to investigate issues discussed in the postmortem
- establishing an annual in-house conference on software process improvement

A True Story

As its postmortem proceeded, one team I worked with became increasingly excited about what it had learned, and wondered how it might spread its mission throughout the company. One senior programmer offered to call the company's CIO, a long-time friend, to talk him into visiting the postmortem on its final day. Although the fact that the project had failed was common knowledge among corporate management—so much so that most of the executives were distancing themselves—the CIO trusted his friend and agreed to a fifteen-minute visit.

Expecting a somber mood when he entered the room, the CIO was visibly startled by the high level of positive energy. Several team members enthusiastically ushered him over to the time line and seismograph. He asked some of the participants to explain the significant points and events, and then sat quietly as another group presented a list of nearly two-dozen lessons mastered during the project. A spokesperson for the group explained that knowing any of these lessons during the project either could have prevented the failure entirely or would have made the issues obvious in enough time for people to take action and save the project. Group members pointed out to the CIO how the rest of the company had not yet learned these lessons, and was still susceptible to failure.

The CIO reflected for a half-second before exclaiming, "You mean I could be sitting on another one of these failures right now?" Everyone nodded.

At the CIO's behest, members of a third group then presented its plan for taking the postmortem lessons company-wide through a series of seminars. They explained that the seminars would be the first in a series of quarterly symposiums presented by in-house staff dedicated to improving software process and quality. The group talked about its wish to form committees to review and improve software practices, to provide relevant training, and to initiate best-practice scouting trips to other local firms to compare notes.

The CIO forgot his quarter-hour limit and spent the next several hours asking questions, contributing ideas, and identifying people he wanted the group to contact. When he asked about cost, no one was able to give him firm numbers, but he remained positive, responding, "I like what I'm hearing. Work up some numbers and run them by me. Assuming we go ahead with this, I'd like a monthly status report on this initiative. And, get in touch with me if you need my help."

To further prove his commitment, the CIO invited the entire team out for dinner, continuing the discussion well into the evening.

Background and theory: The family therapist Virginia Satir has been quoted as saying, "It's not the event that matters, but your reaction to the event." One classic example illustrating the truth in Satir's statement occurred in 1980 when then-President Jimmy Carter realized that the attempt to free the Americans held hostage in Iran had failed. He called a press conference to detail what had happened. In the weeks and months to come, the failed attempt was examined, reexamined, analyzed, and reanalyzed, producing documents filled with information to assure that future attempts made under similar conditions would be successful. President Carter could have tried to deny the action and cover up the truth. However, he chose the response that helped him and the nation grow and learn.

The courage President Carter showed by honestly discussing the failed attempt, and his desire to learn from it, gained him a vast amount of respect. His actions lent credence to the idea that an individual who has suffered a failure has the opportunity to become a respected advocate for change.

A group earns respect when it sponsors honest discussion of what happened, why it happened, and what to do to make sure it doesn't happen again. Publicly sharing the lessons learned with the larger organization transforms the failure into an opportunity for growth. Effective in the political arena, this practice also works well in a business environment in which staff members fear that failure will be punished. A public and honest accounting that helps educate the entire firm can counteract any impulse to punish. The message shared needs to be bold, courageous, and honest, saying, "Don't do as we did. Let's all learn from our experience and make sure that nothing like this happens again."

References for Further Reading

Alinsky, Saul D. *Rules for Radicals: A Primer for Realistic Radicals.* New York: Random House, 1971.

Although it does not teach a person how to become an activist, Alinsky's book deals with ways to guide a group of activists toward a common goal. Throughout his professional life, Alinsky helped establish trade unions and was involved with many other activist efforts. His book contains sage advice for establishing a culture that will help activists achieve their goal.

Boice, Judith L. *The Art of Daily Activism.* Oakland, Calif.: Wingbow Press, 1992.

> Boice introduces readers to a comprehensive way of living life as an activist. Her work is gentle yet strong and somehow convincing. She writes that activism starts with inner work—changing ourselves—and then she addresses changes she as an activist would like made. Read her work to see how she gets her message across, even if you may not agree with her position.

Branden, Nathaniel. *The Six Pillars of Self-Esteem.* New York: Bantam, 1994.

> Branden explains the complex concept of self-esteem simply, first discussing the importance of self-esteem, next detailing each of his "pillars," and then finishing with discussions directed at parents, teachers, and other authority figures. His advice to managers who want to promote self-esteem in the workplace applies well to the facilitation of retrospectives.

Cialdini, Robert B. *Influence: The Psychology of Persuasion.* New York: William Morrow & Co., 1984.

> This text is aimed at marketers, and explains how to influence customers. When I first read the book, I thought the material bordered on the unethical as it seems to describe ways to trick people into buying. I later decided that knowing about the art of persuasion is useful to facilitators, whose job it is to create events

that persuade members of a community to change their ways of operating. The key to ethical use of persuasive material in facilitation is not to define what changes need to be made, but to let the community define what those new ways are. That is, the facilitator's job is to help people get moving in a direction of their own choosing. The "Define Insanity" Exercise is effective because of its use of persuasion. Understanding this, I no longer view Cialdini's advice as outside a reasonable code of ethics.

Kübler-Ross, Elisabeth. *On Death and Dying.* New York: First Collier Books, 1969.

This book, one of several Kübler-Ross wrote on the subject of dying, is the classic that introduces her research and theory to a mass-market audience. Although her scientific work has often been misinterpreted by lay audiences, this book should be read by all facilitators.

Myers, Ware, "Leading from a Powerless Position," *IEEE Software*, Vol. 13, No. 5 (September 1996), pp. 106–8.

In this article based on an interview with me, Ware Myers explores how facilitators can be taught to use the change agent tactics of Gandhi in the workplace setting.

CHAPTER NINE

On Becoming a Skilled Retrospective Facilitator

Bee and Ant long ago had resolved the problem of Ant's dissatisfaction with the beehive condominium, but Ant's difficulties had not ended there. He still had no place to live.

Desperate to relocate, Ant set off in search of a new home, and within days, he found a baby grand piano in a lodge built at the edge of Owl's woods. Without a moment's hesitation, Ant moved in. Living in the piano was like living at a picnic! There was a continuous supply of crumbs dropped by humans having parties, and Ant was a happy camper—except for one thing: He wanted to play the piano but couldn't read a single note!

In hopes of remedying this shortcoming, Ant visited Owl. He knew Owl was not musically inclined, but he thought the wise old bird might be able to recommend a great book. After all, Owl read everything he could get his wings on. Surely, he would help.

Finding Owl asleep in his usual tree, Ant whispered, "Owl, how can I learn to play the piano?"

Owl stirred sleepily, "I don't know. The piano is something I've never tried."

Ant persisted. "Owl, you've learned so much from books. Maybe you can help me find a book that will teach me to play the piano?"

Owl stretched before he responded. "Ant, you can learn great ideas from books, but to put those ideas into practice, you need more than just a book. You need a teacher—and you need to work repeatedly at what you are taught. If you are really interested in playing the piano, why not ask Hummingbird or Nightingale to teach you—music is their life."

Reading a book will only get you part of the way toward your goal, which should be to become the best retrospective facilitator possible. You will also need to work with teachers—to help fine-tune your facilitation techniques, to practice them in safe environments, and to partner with experienced facilitators until you become completely comfortable and proficient in the retrospective setting.

I was not born a skilled facilitator. I was fortunate to be apprenticed—albeit unofficially—by an experienced facilitator named Don Reifer. During my first retrospective, Don and I spent the evenings discussing the days' events. Don explained why he reacted the way he did during each of the sessions.

I practiced my general facilitation skills as a leader of numerous requirements-gathering projects. To learn interpersonal skills, I studied the deeper issues of how people interact. I did this by attending courses geared toward exploring people-related issues as well as courses designed for marriage and family counselors. I also learned interpersonal skills by doing volunteer work for churches and community centers, focusing on environments in which emotions ran high. I assisted counselors leading groups of people in divorce recovery, people coping with the loss of a loved one, and people experiencing the uncertainty and grief of living with a terminally ill spouse.

Through this volunteer work, I came to appreciate that positive learning occurs when people are able to express their emotions. I used this realization to improve my skills as a facilitator. During retrospectives, when emotions surfaced, I learned to not shy away from exploring the story behind those emotions. At the same time, I learned to respect a person's right to keep his or her thoughts private. I never force participants to explore a topic if they don't want to. Remember, for a retrospective to feel safe, *everything must be optional,* including the discussion of feelings.

SIX LESSONS

My earliest retrospectives involved successful projects with teams whose members had worked well together. Over time, as I became more experienced, I led retrospectives of unsuccessful projects, dealing with increasingly serious problems. I partnered with experienced facilitators every chance I could. Through their instruction and through the school of hard knocks, I have learned valuable lessons, which I share below.

Lesson 1: Manage current topic, flow of ideas, and quality.

Acquiring basic facilitation skills is a must for anyone intent on leading retrospectives, but advice on exactly how to go about acquiring the skills is beyond the scope of this book. My Website (www.retrospectives.com) suggests courses that can be taken by fledgling facilitators, but newcomers to the skill set may find it useful to keep three fundamental rules in mind.

1. Make sure that everyone knows what is being talked about, and that all are talking about the same thing.

2. Channel the flow of ideas to keep people focused and to keep abreast of people's moods.

3. Maintain a high standard for the quality of discussion.

Rule 1: Make sure that everyone knows what is being talked about, and that all are talking about the same thing. A retrospective involves different minds processing a vast amount of new information and attempting to reconcile that information with past experiences. It is natural for people to become distracted and lose track of what the group is trying to accomplish, or for the team to forget the goal of an exercise.

One of your jobs is to accept that people will go off on tangents, and then bring them back to the current goals and objectives of the exercise. As tangential topics surface, you will need to be patient and not take offense. The conversation does not mean that they are not listening to you, but rather that you are causing them to think about something new and to learn. I maintain my patience first by consciously relaxing, and then by reminding myself that the digression is really a compliment. It's an indication that I'm doing my job!

Rule 2: Channel the flow of ideas to keep people focused and to keep abreast of people's moods. Put twenty or so people in a room with no guidelines to structure their interaction, and you have a party. Ideas flow everywhere. Naturally gifted speakers will talk easily and frequently and may try to engage their colleagues in discussion; others, who might be gifted *thinkers*, may spend their time reflecting on what they are hearing. One beauty of being human is that we are all different. However, without structure or a format, some people may talk too much (and sometimes say very little!) while others won't be able to get a word in.

It is the facilitator's job to ensure that everyone has an equal opportunity to speak, while moving each discussion toward a resolution. "Equal opportunity" does not mean that everyone *must* speak, but that when someone wants to, he or she can. I try to create an environment in which conversation is natural and free-flowing. If too many people want to talk, I generally announce, "I'm going to play traffic cop now," adding that I will only respond to raised hands. As traffic cop, I stand near the center of the room and silently point to people who have their hands up to let them know that I've seen them and that they are second, third, and so on, in line to speak.

Another objective of channeling the flow of ideas involves helping the community reach closure and move on. If I hear a conversation that goes around in circles or delves into vast amounts of history with no resolution in sight, I stop the discussion and ask people to formulate a conclusion. I might ask, "What conclusion or lesson can I record here?" or, if no conclusion is forthcoming, I might suggest a conclusion and ask, "Is that close?" Soon, participants in the retrospective or post-mortem realize that every discussion needs to end in some sort of learning to be captured on a flip chart, and they begin to steer themselves toward that goal.

Channeling the flow of ideas also helps me to read the mood of the participants to see whether anyone needs a break, or to assess whether people's energy is waning on the particular exercise, indicating that we should shift to another one. Throughout the sessions, I observe body language to monitor people's physical and mental states, but I always test my instincts and observations before I act upon them. I might say, "It looks to me as if some of you need a break. Am I right?" If no one supports my observation, I ask people to fill me in on what else is going on. Usually, this little bit of intervention clears the way to closure.

Rule 3: Maintain a high standard for the quality of discussion. This task involves listening to what is said and making sure all discussions confirm that group members show each other complete respect during discussions, that they espouse as truth the statement that "we did the best we could, given what we knew at the time," and that everyone remembers that the goal is to learn how to improve.

As I listen, I am on guard especially for any jokes or cutting remarks made at the expense of someone else on the team or in the room. If I hear any, I stop the discussion, remind the group of our fundamental ground rules, and encourage an apology if necessary.

In addition, I listen for ineffective communication—coded or garbled messages, partial messages, or messages tainted with blame, guilt, or the like. In such cases, I help the speaker rethink and rephrase his or her ideas so that any appropriate message is conveyed without hindrance.

Lesson 2: Ask for help when you need it.

On occasion, I accept a retrospective for which my skills turn out to be inadequate. I learned early to be able to admit that I was in trouble and to ask for help. Every time I've asked for assistance, I've found someone—a colleague, a consultant, or even a participant in the retrospective itself—who could help me turn the situation around.

Although it is key to be able to ask for help, one must also be careful to maintain a network of contacts who are available to serve as emergency lifelines. Just knowing you have someone you can call for advice reduces anxiety and increases your effectiveness.

Lesson 3: Avoid triangulation.

There are times when someone in a retrospective relates something to me off-the-record about a third party. He or she may want to explain what this colleague thinks or why the person reacts in a particular way, or he or she may be trying to make me a confidante to take sides in some external exchange.

I've learned to listen to the information, but not necessarily to accept it at face value, or act on it. I try to redirect this conversation as it should occur between the speaker and the third party. I ask whether the speaker has discussed the topic with the other person. If the answer is no, I explore how a dialogue might be initiated. If the answer is yes, I question what the speaker hopes to accomplish by confiding in me. Usually, my demeanor and guidance enable the speaker to take proper action to rectify the situation.

I work hard to maintain my role as a neutral third party. By reminding myself and others that my job is to facilitate discussion and learning, not to pass judgment or attempt to "fix" anything or anyone in the community, I keep the retrospective on track.

A True Story

During a break in a retrospective, Fred, the manager, thought his senior technical lead, Mike, was contributing "too much, as he always does." It was early in the retrospective and I didn't think Mike's participation was out of line. Instead, I found Fred's comment curious. I asked more about it and found that Fred felt Mike was holding back the growth of the junior developers by always having an answer. When I asked Fred if he had mentioned his concern to Mike, he said, "No, I fear Mike might be insulted" and he admitted that he didn't know how to proceed.

I arranged to have lunch with both Mike and Fred. When the discussion turned to team maturity, I asked, "Mike, if there were things you could do to improve team members' growth, how would you like to hear about them?"

A bit exasperated, Mike replied, "Norm, just tell me."

"Suppose team members had a similar message, how would you like to hear it?"

More exasperated, Mike said, "Then they should just tell me."

"Would that also hold for Fred?"

"Yep."

I turned to Fred and said, "I think we both would like to hear what you have to say."

The rest of the lunch conversation was magical. Mike learned that Fred thought he was trying too hard and was condescending when the junior developers contributed an idea. Fred learned that early in the project when everyone decided Mike "was dominating and touchy," Mike was actually caring for his dying parent—and was therefore reasonably out-of-sorts. Now time had passed and Mike was frustrated because he felt he was in a "dome of silence." No one else contributed when he was around—he had to do it all himself.

Mike and Fred finished lunch with a new respect for each other. Simultaneously, they commented, "We need to talk honestly more often."

Lesson 4: See things from a systems perspective.

When I encounter a situation that seems to make no sense, I search for the bigger picture. For example, members of a community may look at an event or a decision and misinterpret the intent, resulting in deadlocked discussion and review. Most frequently, this occurs when people are looking at the matter solely from their own point of view—a distortion that can be remedied by directing them to see where the problem fits within a whole-system perspective.

At other times, an individual may appear to be the source of the deadlock. I once facilitated a retrospective in which one woman was accused of not being a team player, of trying to impose academic theory in the real world, and of being obsessed with process. She was labeled as a complainer because she wanted better specifications, better and increased interaction with the customers, a way to ensure needed change and version control, and testing procedures that would not be sacrificed in order to deliver the system earlier.

She was viewed as *the* problem by the whole community—but, in reality, she was the only one willing to stand up and say,

"Our approach to building software needs work," and she was right!

By freeing the group to look beyond a single perspective to the whole system, the facilitator can move the community to a new level of learning and understanding.

Lesson 5: Seek first to understand, and then to be understood.

In *The Seven Habits of Highly Effective People,* Stephen Covey advocates that we learn to *really* listen to what a person is trying to say. It is easy for me to assume that I know what the speaker intends and then to try to manage the group's discussion based on my own experience and assumptions, only to discover later an interesting twist that I hadn't anticipated!

Over the years, I have learned first to listen and then to ask questions in order to understand the speaker's perspective. Sometimes, my initial conclusions are correct, and I could have jumped ahead and explained the issue to the group. However, careful articulation of the problem is important if group members themselves are going to be able to understand the issues well enough to arrive at a solution. Offering a solution while most of the community is still trying to understand the problem does not work.

The most effective approach to problem solving is to enable members of the retrospective community to discover their own answers. Sometimes, they arrive at the solution I expect. Sometimes, they find a better one. By asking more questions and giving fewer answers, the facilitator helps the team to assure future success.

Lesson 6: When something isn't working, try something different.

Jerry Weinberg's *The Secrets of Consulting* introduced me to what seems now to be an obvious but brilliant idea: If you are in the middle of holding an exercise or participating in a discussion and progress is not being made, then try something different! It doesn't matter so much what you try, since what you are currently doing isn't working, but that you make a change.

How do I determine what to try? In such situations, I'll think through past experiences to see whether there is anything that might work. If not, I'll trust my intuition. Usually, my gut feelings will lead me to the invention of a new exercise. Trusting your creativity is important. Sometimes, I'll start a new exercise without knowing exactly where it will lead, but I always let people know we are trying something new. If it doesn't work, we move to another exercise or approach.

Sometimes, people react negatively to my suggestion of inventing something new, perhaps because it scares them to have no plan and little idea of where they are going. Veteran facilitators especially seem wary of trying something radically new, believing it is the facilitator's responsibility to be in control of the retrospective. My response is that this belief is valid, but that successful facilitation depends on one's view of "control." Trying something new to help a community move past a barrier seems to me to be an example both of good facilitating and of good leading.

I suspect that many a facilitator's fear of trying the unknown comes from a lack of experience as well as a lack of confidence. (If one tries new things, one will fail sometimes and succeed at other times. By trying, you discover you can recover.) Long ago, I studied improvisational comedy with a group called ComedySportz. The lessons helped me become comfortable with leading "in the moment," trying something—anything—even if I don't believe I'm good at it or don't know what I'm doing. Through improvisation, I learned to try new approaches while listening and reacting to my audience's response. Another way to build confidence that you can venture into the unknown, survive, and even succeed beyond your expectations is through organizations that promote public speaking. The Toastmasters organization has an exercise called "table topics," in which people speak extemporaneously on a topic. These techniques won't guarantee you'll pick the best "something different" to try when what you've been doing is not working, but they will lend a boldness and confidence to your manner—an attitude that can prove catching!

Understanding the Facilitator's Procedures

As programmers, we use the word *procedure* all the time, but I don't think we appreciate the power of the word beyond the context of programming. One dictionary tells us that a procedure is a series of steps taken to accomplish an end.

Think how a surgeon uses this word. During an operation, a surgeon might select a procedure from his vast mental collection to solve a particular situation he or she discovers—usually in real-time.

As a retrospective facilitator, I've collected a number of retrospective procedures, stored in my mind and ready for use when an applicable situation arises. These procedures are not retrospective exercises any more than a single medical procedure is an operation. Nevertheless, I may use one or more of these procedures to help a particular exercise run more effectively. Similarly, I may use a single procedure in more than one exercise during the same retrospective, if that is what the situation calls for.

In the remainder of this chapter, I list commonly used procedures that I use while leading a retrospective.

The "Dealing with Conflict" Procedure

There are times when a retrospective gets bogged down by a conflict. As with most battles, we expect that one side in the conflict will win and the other will lose, but as long as those involved see winning and losing as the only possible outcomes, the conflict will remain unresolved. Whenever preexisting or new conflict situations arise, I employ a tailored conflict-resolving approach.

Basic Concept

Facilitating resolution of a preexisting conflict involves several steps that you can take:

Step 1: State that conflict, as such, is neither bad nor good, but is simply a fact of life. Within conflict, opportunities for discovery or invention exist that can lead to a better solution than either party might have initially imagined. When this optimism is expressed to groups in conflict, it usually arouses their curiosity and helps them begin to move away from the source of conflict itself.

Step 2: Ask both parties whether they want to work on resolving the conflict. Explain that the process involves looking at the events leading up to the conflict and at alternative resolutions, and tell them they'll need to abandon their current position for a time. Let them know, however, that they are free to return to their current position at the end of the process. Try to sense whether the participants are serious about searching for a solution. If they are not, then stop your intervention—you can't help them if not everyone wants to solve the conflict. In most cases, they will be serious and will want to move forward.

Step 3: Explore the two parties' different positions by asking them to articulate their goals, fears, concerns, intentions, and desires. It's quite possible that each party arrived at its position without fully understanding how it got there. Because the goal of this discussion is understanding, not the passing of judgment, all parties need to hear their own and their opponent's reasons—and then honor these beliefs as valid for the owning party. When all issues are understood (but not necessarily accepted) by all parties, move to the next step.

Step 4: Review each party's statements and interests and identify issues that are common to more than one party. Finding interests or goals that opposing parties share might take some creativity (for example, try restating the matter from a different slant) but it can be done, and it is a way to build common understanding among parties. This is often enough to resolve a conflict; in the best of cases, a proposed solution might be offered and accepted rather quickly. If it is not, proceed with identifying issues that are not common, being careful to establish how important each of them is to the owning party. Then, move to the next step.

Step 5: Involve all participants in finding new solutions. These must be solutions that have not been proposed before, which take into account everyone's motivations and concerns. If you have rated the issues according to importance, you might first explore solutions that address all the important factors before you see whether the parties are willing to drop less important issues. If high-quality solutions are not identified, give participants some time to think quietly by themselves. Do this by stopping the session and resuming at a later time.

Step 6: List all possible solutions that at least partially resolve the conflict and have the community evaluate and select the most satisfactory candidate. Then, ask each party whether it wants to return to its previous position. Participants are usually ready to proceed with the new jointly developed solution.

Applied to Retrospectives

When a conflict arises *during* a retrospective, you have two choices: Either you can help resolve the conflict immediately, or you can observe that the conflict is beyond the scope of the retrospective. In the second case, you'll want to refer the conflict as a topic for special handling, and move on to other issues. If you choose the second approach, add the issue of resolving the conflict to the community's "to do" list. All action to help resolve the conflict, whether overseen by you or another party, should be conducted *after* completion of the current retrospective.

Factors to consider include the following:

Time constraints:	Conflict resolution takes time. You may take the retrospective irrevocably off-schedule by taking on the challenge.
Magnitude:	Small conflicts can easily be resolved within a retrospective, while larger ones (with more history) may take more time than is available.
Personality:	Sometimes, the conflict is not about an issue, but rather reflects a power struggle between opposing parties. If this is the case, then the topic of the power struggle is what needs to be addressed. You might use one of the retrospective exercises to bring this issue to light, such as the "Making the Magic Happen" Exercise, in which you say, "I want to talk about the one topic we haven't yet discussed."
Resolution training:	If conflict is common within the community's way of working, then teaching people how to resolve conflict might be valuable. You can demonstrate it within the retrospective, or arrange for a different time to present such a session. If conflict resolution is an issue for just a few individuals, then you might want to address the conflict outside of the retrospective.

References for Further Reading

Fisher, Roger, and William Ury. *Getting to Yes*. New York: Penguin Books, 1981.

This book introduces the process behind the six steps discussed above in the Basic Concept section. An easy-to-read book, it gives a great deal of practical advice on how to work through polarized positions.

Crum, Thomas F. *The Magic of Conflict.* New York: Simon & Schuster, 1987.

Crum discusses dealing with conflict from a philosophical point of view, and provides a discussion of how people can live their ordinary lives and still be at peace within the world.

Hocker, Joyce L., and William W. Wilmot. *Interpersonal Conflict,* 3rd ed. Madison, Wisc.: Wm. C. Brown Publishers, 1991.

Hocker and Wilmot present a comprehensive treatment of the subject of conflict. Used in university courses on mediation, the book surveys various theories on how to handle conflict, covering the material in greater depth than can be taught during a retrospective, but at a level that is valuable for a facilitator to have mastered.

The "Handling Resistance to Change" Procedure

Someone once asked me how I deal with resistance to change in an organization. My reply was, "I don't find resistance to change to be a problem." It wasn't until much later that it dawned on me that I *handle resistance to change by not seeing it as a problem.*

Instead, I see resistance as a carrier providing information about a person's thinking process and I use it as an opener for more dialogue. Whoever coined the phrase, "You can't teach an old dog new tricks" didn't know how people learn! Although it is true that children generally embrace new ideas and activities, adults show varying degrees of acceptance or of reluctance. Resistance to new ideas is very natural. The behavior shows that an individual is actively engaged in evaluating the new possibilities against his or her past experiences. This mapping of new ideas onto past experiences is a fundamental part of adult learning. I, for example, have conditioned myself to respond to resistance as if it is an invitation to participate in this mapping.

When someone resists a change, it is usually for one of two reasons:

- The individual is trying to avoid some pain that he or she thinks will come if the new way of working is adopted.
- The person is trying to prevent something that is positive and enjoyable in the current situation from being lost by the new way of working.

If you realize that resistance to change is due to an interest in either avoiding pain or maintaining joy, you can ask specific questions in order to better understand the motivation behind the resistance—and thereby help people to move beyond it. There is a two-step approach that can be taken: It involves discovery first and then a coaching-and-learning effort.

Basic Concept

> *Step 1: Determine what the resisting individual is avoiding or protecting.* The key attributes a facilitator needs to express in this step are patience, careful listening, and taking a position not associated with a specific outcome.

> *Step 2: Work with the resisting individual to discover ways to help him or her avoid the pain or maintain the joy in the new way of working.* In some cases, this means learning more about a topic so the participant feeling the conflict realizes that whatever he or she wants to avoid or maintain is satisfactorily addressed in the new way of working. In other cases, it means modifying the intended changes to make them compatible with those required by the resisting individual.

Both the discovery-oriented first step and the coaching-and-learning second step may require more than one discussion session. Many people learn by alternating cycles in which they think quietly on their own with those in which they discuss matters openly with a group of peers. In the discussion part of the cycle, people often will talk about all aspects of the intended change, including any negative feelings they have. The comment, "This change is inappropriate because . . ." is not a threat to the intended change, but rather part of the learning process.

Applied to Retrospectives

Discussing the future usually leads to proposing change. As the discussion occurs, I listen for comments that might give me clues about the pain that people fear or the joy they value. I help them articulate their concerns, and challenge the teams proposing change to address those concerns. I create time-outs in the various exercises and ask people first to think quietly, and then to write about the proposed changes on a card or in a journal. I follow this activity with discussion, breaking the community into small groups, working with the whole community, or sometimes meeting only with individuals as part of my follow-up after the retrospective.

The "Four Freedoms" Procedure

Every now and then, as you prepare for a retrospective, you may encounter workers who believe themselves to be disempowered. One reason for the feeling may be that the workers don't know how to take charge of matters themselves and believe that their organization has deliberately disempowered them. They may be misinterpreting the motivation behind such legitimate management endeavors as information-seeking or project-control activities. Another possibility is that managers actually have unintentionally disempowered workers. In rare cases, management may intentionally seek to disempower workers, but I don't know much about these environments, since the organizations that foster them don't hold retrospectives!

Most managers learn to manage on the job with little or no training, and may have incorporated practices that make sense from their point of view but not from the workers' perspective. Or, they may simply be unaware of the implications of the specific practices to their workers. With either of these two situations, the "Four Freedoms"can help.

Basic Concept

The "Four Freedoms" are universally found in all empowered workplaces:

1. You have the freedom to talk about the project the way you see it, rather than the way others want you to see it.

2. You have the freedom to ask about any puzzles.

3. You have the freedom to talk about whatever is coming up for you.

4. You have the freedom to say that you don't really feel you have one or more of the preceding three freedoms.

These four freedoms are deceptively simple but effective. That you have the *freedom to talk about the project the way you see it* gives permission to you along with everyone else to speak about the project. Sometimes, people are afraid to say what's really going on for fear that they will be labeled disloyal, complainers, or whistle-blowers. This freedom gives everyone the opportunity—and the responsibility—to say, "We are off schedule and will not easily get back on." It is this kind of input that managers need to hear in order to effectively manage their projects.

The *freedom to ask about any puzzles* allows anyone to ask for information about the project. Many times, people will go about their work without understanding how the pieces of the project fit together. Puzzles—actions or events that don't make sense to everyone—might derive from bad ideas or from simple oversight. Conversely, they might be clues identifying misunderstood goals, or great but poorly communicated ideas. Because there are some questions that won't be answered (such as "When are we going public?" or "How large was Fred's raise?"), *empowerment* does not necessarily mean getting the answers to all questions, but rather means being able to ask for information that helps you do the job.

The *freedom to talk about whatever is coming up for you* allows people to talk about feelings of excitement, happiness, concern, fear, uneasiness, discomfort, or interest, for example. In many environments, it is neither easy nor encouraged to talk about feelings, even though such discussions can provide crucial information about the project. I use the phrase "whatever comes up for you," instead of the word "feelings" to disarm the hesitancy some people have with discussing their workplace feelings.

The *freedom to say that you don't really feel you have one or more of the preceding three freedoms* is listed because people make mistakes. If managers are under stress, they may not respond well to someone exercising one of these freedoms. Or, when someone abuses a freedom—using one at the wrong time; using one to embarrass, distract, or delay; or even using a freedom to complain, for example—the natural reaction on the part of management may be to discount, ignore, or punish the behavior. Whatever the case, the fourth freedom reminds us that all parties need to discuss the freedoms, learn how to use them, and learn how to respond appropriately to someone else using them.

Applied to Retrospectives

I use the "Four Freedoms" wherever I see a need for them. Prework and one-on-one interviews can give you clues about trouble spots. In some cases, I may decide to offer the "Four Freedoms" to one individual, but more often, I offer them to an entire group experiencing unintentional disempowerment.

A True Story

All the testers in the quality-assurance group submitted pre-work that suggested they were disempowered. I telephoned each of the testers and arranged to have dinner with the entire group before the retrospective started. During the dinner, I asked what kinds of topics people hoped would be covered. As the discussion proceeded, I stated that I would not be responsible for bringing these topics to light; the testers would need to speak out. I further commented that I would be willing to state my observation that a number of topics, which previously had been discussed privately, had not been brought up. In response to this comment, the testers explained that discussing those topics wouldn't be safe.

I then offered the "Four Freedoms" and asked group members to tell me what would make them feel comfortable enough to exercise their freedoms. "Permission from the project manager!" they all replied. Later, I asked the project manager for permission, which he immediately granted. Almost as an afterthought, he commented, "I'd love it if the testers would start speaking up. I don't know why they don't."

During the opening session of the retrospective, I added the "Four Freedoms" to the statement of ground rules and then asked the whole community—testers, analysts, and developers alike—to agree to try them. They willingly agreed, but during the following days, there were a few times when I had to encourage the use of the freedoms. By the end of the retrospective, however, a new norm had been established. The experience began an organizational tradition of proactive testers that continues today.

I use the "Four Freedoms" method in situations such as the preceding, but I also may elect to use it when a "Session Without Managers" Exercise is requested. This request suggests to me that the work environment is one in which some people feel they don't have their four freedoms. When the "Session Without Managers" is scheduled, I introduce the "Four Freedoms" as ground rules to be used throughout the retrospective. This allows people to practice the freedoms during the time that I'm available to keep discussions safe and on track.

References for Further Reading

Gause, Donald C., and Gerald M. Weinberg. *Exploring Requirements: Quality Before Design.* New York: Dorset House Publishing, 1989.

> The discussion of the art of being fully present, which appears on page 140, was instrumental in my discovering what I call the "Four Freedoms." However, my discovery came about because of my *mis*interpretation of the material! Nevertheless, the positive result was my invention of this method.

Satir, Virginia. *Making Contact.* Berkeley, Calif.: Celestial Arts, 1976.

> Satir discusses five freedoms that are the natural birthright of all human beings. Her freedoms do not parallel my "Four Freedoms," but it will be obvious to students of Satir that I was influenced both by her freedoms and the community-building tools.

The "Understanding Differences in Preferences" Procedure

During a retrospective, differences in the way people go about their work will become apparent. Type theory fosters the study of these differences to uncover patterns to enable us to better understand and appreciate each other. While there are numerous systems that explain differences in people, one of the most researched and validated is the Myers-Briggs' Temperament Types system.

Basic Concept

Myers-Briggs is a system that studies our natural preferences for problem solving. Using this system, we look at four aspects of problem solving and identify the preferences we have. For example, as we search for a solution to a problem,

1. Do we prefer to *interact with others*, such as in a brainstorming session, or do we prefer to *work solo*, with only our thoughts to concern us?

2. Do we prefer to acquire information relevant to solving the problem through use of our *five senses* or by relying on our *intuition?*

3. What filters do we use to sift through all the information we have collected about a problem that help us identify important information and lead us toward a solution? Do we prefer *abstract* concepts (theories, logic, and the like) or are we interested in *interactions among people* (relationships and feelings)?

4. How much information do we need to support a difficult decision and how comfortable are we before and after the decision is made? Do we prefer to *seek closure* or to *keep options open* as we collect more information?

The Myers-Briggs system looks at preferences, not at skills and ability. Presumably, most people have the skills and ability to problem-solve from any of the preferences mentioned above. However, for each of the four scenarios each of us prefers one of the two possibilities.

Given that we each have our own preferences and that only rarely are we aware of other people's preferences, it is easy for us to assume that everyone goes about solving problems in the same way we do. At play during group problem-solving sessions and affecting team interactions, these different preferences can cause interesting conflicts.

A full discussion of Myers-Briggs is beyond the scope of this book, but this brief introduction should alert you to the importance of the material. I encourage you to study it as thoroughly as you can.

Applied to Retrospectives

As I observe the community, I use type theory to help me understand why participants may not be working well together. Typical type-related situations include

- An entire team is composed of one dominant type, and regularly misses opportunities to solve problems because of the limited number of problem-solving approaches available to it.
- Most of a team is composed of one type, but includes a few disenfranchised individuals whom the majority does not understand.
- A team is composed of two subgroup types, each with its own preferences; neither understands the other's behavior.

By understanding the behavior type that a team has adopted as its natural problem-solving approach, I can tailor my assignments to take advantage of the team's preferences, or to help its members try a new approach. For example, if a team's natural preference is to work in a brainstorming session, and I want to help members try a different approach, I ask them to write instead of talk.

Here is another example. If some members prefer to seek closure and others need to keep their options open until they've had the chance for further reflection, I adapt exercises to identify "candidate" solutions, and then tell the group that we will revisit each possible solution later, choosing one after we have had a chance to absorb the details of each option.

Even though my job is to facilitate a retrospective, not to fix a group, I may offer suggestions on how a group might improve staff relations. In communities in which Myers-Briggs has been introduced, I may use Myers-Briggs vocabulary to explain baffling interactions. Type theory is well known in Personnel/Human Resources departments and it is possible that the community has been introduced to it. However, it is rare for casual students of the system to remember the details of type or terminology, or to have mastered it.

A True Story

A team I worked with was composed almost entirely of people who preferred to keep their options open. They had long discussions that looked at all aspects of a topic, and frequently returned to previous discussions to be sure they were on the right path. However, one person on the team preferred to seek closure, and was frustrated by discussions that went on seemingly forever. I asked team members to assign the job of timekeeper to that person, and suggested that they all work together to design ground rules for timekeeping.

They formulated ground rules, as follows: At the beginning of each discussion, they would agree on how long it would last; when the time was up, the timekeeper would interrupt. Team members would then either close the discussion and reach a decision, or determine what else they needed to do before they could reach closure. They would then set a new time limit.

Team members continued to use their system after the retrospective was over. It became such a habit that when the timekeeper went on maternity leave, she left the team with a kitchen timer to use until she returned. They laughed at the joke, but a few days later they needed to use it!

References for Further Reading

Keirsey, David, and Marilyn Bates. *Please Understand Me: Character & Temperament Types,* 4th ed. Del Mar, Calif.: Prometheus Nemesis Book Co., 1984.

Keirsey and Bates do an excellent job of introducing Myers-Briggs Type Indicator and Temperament Type theories. Their book includes discussion of how these types influence leadership as well as of how they apply in day-to-day interactions with family and friends.

Kroeger, Otto, with Janey Thuesen. *Type Talk at Work.* New York: Delacorte Press, 1992.

This is a good book to read after you've read Keirsey and Bates. It addresses using type theory in the workplace, including ethical uses and abuses. The authors include suggestions on how to work with people of different types and how to build an effective team.

The "Ingredients of an Interaction" Procedure

Communication can go astray for all sorts of reasons. A listener misunderstands a word, remembers a similar conversation from the past and misinterprets the new message, or concludes how the message will end before the speaker has even finished. The list of reasons for communication problems is endless. In a retrospective, communication becomes more difficult if listeners are under stress; their listening skills may flag or collapse entirely. To be effective, a facilitator must first recognize that a message has gone astray and then know how to get the discussion back on track. One way I do this is by identifying and utilizing what I call *the ingredients of an interaction.*

Basic Concept

Before I reveal the procedure, let me provide a bit of background, which comes from both Virginia Satir and Jerry Weinberg. In the four volumes of *Quality Software Management,* Weinberg interprets Satir's Interaction Model for a software engineering audience. *Volume 2,* especially, uses the model to show how a listener passes a message through several stages before he or she can fully understand and respond to it. At each stage, the listener engages in important analysis of the message. Weinberg's treatment of the topic is comprehensive and edifying—and might well be read in its entirety—but I have developed a condensed and paraphrased version to use as a facilitation tool, as follows.

- *Stage 1: Intake.* The listener analyzes what he or she saw and heard about the message.

- *Stage 2: Assign a meaning.* The listener determines a meaning using the analysis from the intake stage.

- *Stage 3: Determine a feeling.* The listener develops a feeling in response to the message (for example, he or she feels hurt, disappointed, proud, surprised, confused, or some other emotion) based on intake and meaning.

- *Stage 4: Identify a feeling about the feeling.* After the listener has identified the initial feeling, he or she reacts to the feeling. For example, if the listener has been paid a compliment and feels proud, how does he or she feel about feeling proud? Embarrassed, ashamed, or complimented are all possible emotions and these may color how he or she responds to the message.

Each of the four stages adds to the process of how a listener understands a message and prepares a response. Messages become confused when a listener either misinterprets or skips one or more of the four stages. Success in the final stage, shown below, is dependent on the first four stages of analysis.

- *Stage 5: Develop a response.* The listener formulates a response. If the listener has high self-esteem, and hears a message that is confusing, he or she probably will ask for clarification in order to discover whether any part of the analysis is incorrect. But if the listener has low self-esteem, his or her response may be inappropriate, confused, or ineffective. Such a person may feel unsafe, showing this distress by perhaps becoming either combative or uncharacteristically quiet.

Applied to Retrospectives

As facilitator, you can use the preceding five-stage model to help redirect communication that has gone astray. If someone responds in a way that doesn't make sense, stop and ask what might have happened. Perhaps the listener processed the message incorrectly, but in the most extreme of conflicts, you can find out exactly what's happening by stopping the dialogue, asking the speaker to repeat the message, and walking the listener through each of the five stages. In such a case, be careful to document the processing and explore alternative conclusions with the listener. I don't intervene in this fashion very often, since my job is to facilitate the retrospective, not to fix individual listening skills, and I generally avoid direct and lengthy intervention. Instead, I use the five-stage model for my own understanding, and find other ways to resolve miscommunication among team members.

References for Further Reading

Satir, Virginia, John Banmen, Jane Gerber, and Maria Gomori. *The Satir Model, Family Therapy and Beyond.* Palo Alto, Calif.: Science and Behavior Books, 1991.

> Satir developed a complex model for understanding what goes on in another's head. Satir's Interaction Model explains feedback loops, family rules, and covert and overt responses based on levels of self-esteem. Written for an audience of fully trained family therapists, Satir's work is brilliant but decidedly difficult. I recommend that it be tackled after the Weinberg text listed in the next entry.

Weinberg, Gerald M. *Quality Software Management: Vol. 2, First-Order Measurement.* New York: Dorset House Publishing, 1993.

> In this book, Weinberg develops a model to explain Satir's work in the context of software management.

The Satir Interaction Model is such an important tool for understanding communication that most of Weinberg's book is dedicated to its many facets. I use Weinberg's material not just in retrospectives but throughout the software projects I lead. When you think of all the possible communication that occurs during a software project, and realize the implications if any of it goes astray, you will understand why I believe all facilitators should master this material.

The "Congruent Messages" Procedure

A retrospective provides the opportunity for a community to share stories about a past project. Many of these stories are easily told and easily received, but a few are exceedingly difficult. They are difficult because they involve pain, frustration, fear, and other emotions that make people feel weak and vulnerable. When these feelings arise and our messages are adversely affected by our emotions, we may communicate mixed messages, which have overtones that can compromise the success of a retrospective. It is important for a facilitator to recognize these inappropriate messages, to measure the resulting tension among group members, and to intervene in order to help the speaker reword his or her message so that it is accurate and likely to be understood.

Basic Concept

Virginia Satir's writings describe effective styles of communication as *congruent* and styles that cause difficulty as *incongruent.* Satir uses the word "congruent" for messages whose content matches the speaker's thoughts and body language.

According to Satir, a congruent message has three components, which Jerry Weinberg calls Observer Positions in the *Quality Software Management* series. In the following, I summarize these components—positions from which to observe what people need to work on in a conflict.

1. *Self* is the position that honors your right to think and feel as you do about a situation.
2. *Other* is the position that recognizes that another person, who is receiving your message, also has the right to feel and think about a situation in his or her own way.
3. *Context* is the position that enables you to share the details of the situation as accurately and as honestly as possible.

To illustrate the effect of congruence, let's imagine that the following message is delivered during a retrospective by a testing specialist talking to a software developer:

"When you gave us Release 1.0 of the new system, it had not been entered into the configuration management system— pieces of the system resided on several programmers' machines. These pieces were continually changing, as last-minute features were added.

"As a result, we tested software that was obsolete. We were hurt to find out that we had spent our limited time identifying defects that had already been removed, and that we were testing code while at the same time you were introducing new defects. Our defect reports were ignored, and the effort we spent testing was wasted. It made us feel as if our jobs were pointless.

"I understand that you need to add as many features as time allows, but we need a more disciplined change process from you. I want to talk about what is possible."

In this exchange, the *Self* was included when the speaker explained how the testing team felt about wasting its time. The *Other* was included by the speaker's recognition that the development group needed to add features at the last minute, and by the invitation to discuss what was possible. The concept of *Context* was included when the testing specialist described having problems with the software change process.

Incongruent Messages

In addition to the three components, the work of Virginia Satir identifies four common styles of *incongruent message*. Each of these ineffective message styles occurs because one or more of the three components of a congruent message has been left out. Note that it's not specific *words* that are left out, but rather the components of *Self*, *Other*, and *Context*. Because Jerry Weinberg also treats this topic well (see especially *Quality Software Management, Vol. 3*), I've compressed his wisdom with Satir's to derive my version.

Style 1: Blaming. If the *Other* component is left out, the message becomes a blaming style of incongruent message. The message might take the following form:

"You sure made our lives miserable when you gave us Release 1.0. While we were working overtime to make sure that the software was the best it could be, you were changing all parts of the system. The software was not in the configuration management system, so you couldn't even tell us what had changed! There was no way we could know what needed to be tested again, or to know what defects you had already repaired. You made us waste our time, and we don't like it."

This message was created with no awareness that software developers have any responsibilities other than to keep testers happy. It does not include an offer to work together to try to find common ground between the different positions, goals, and needs.

A blaming style is ineffective in many ways. The message above might result in the developers using the configuration management system, but at a cost. The developers may react to the blamer by trying to get even or by withholding information during further interactions to avoid being blamed again.

The message might also cause the software developers to take a stand to defend their decision not to use the configuration management system. In such a case, we would be left with two polarized groups fighting about configuration management, and demonstrating no interest in working together to improve their software process.

Style 2: Placating. Another kind of incongruent style involves leaving *Self* out of the message. Here is an example:

"It was very difficult to test Release 1.0. Things kept changing and we were not very good at knowing what we should test and what we should retest. The software developers have such an important job adding all the features they can before the software ships. We understand that they don't have time to use a configuration management system. I guess we need to do something different in testing."

In the placating style of incongruence, the speaker ignores all of his or her feelings and thoughts on the subject, and delivers the message so that it will not upset the listener. In so doing, the speaker appears to be accepting total responsibility for a situation when it should be shared.

A placating style is ineffective because it leaves listeners with the impression that they don't need to do anything about the situation. They conclude that the speaker will take responsibility for solving the problem.

In the message above, the speaker is hoping that the software development group will realize its foolishness at not using the configuration management system and will volunteer to change. This type of change almost never happens.

Style 3: Super-Reasonable. A third style of incongruence, which I see quite often in the high-tech community, is called super-reasonable. In this style, both *Self* and *Other* are left out of the message. The only thing left in the message is *Context*. This yields a message that sounds like it came from *Star Trek's* Mr. Spock. For example:

> "It is known that the lack of using a configuration management system yields difficulties for a testing function. These difficulties include wasted testing resources and missed opportunities to discover defects. It is estimated that the cost to this project was an efficiency loss of 61 percent."

A super-reasonable style avoids discussion of anyone's feelings or position. The message includes facts and nothing else, often containing statistics that are not particularly accurate and that provide no truly useful information. There is no suggestion of what needs to be done.

This style is ineffective because, after the message has been delivered, no one knows what to do next. The author of the message hasn't given the recipients a clue about what he or she thinks should happen, nor has the author invited the recipients to discuss how to resolve the problem.

Style 4: Irrelevance. The fourth style of incongruence involves shifting the topic away from the real issue. In this case, *Self*, *Other*, and *Context* have all been removed from the message. People who are really good at this style often turn it into humor, and may be appreciated because they help the group avoid talking about the difficult issues. An example of this type of message follows:

> "This project really required us to be quick on our feet. Things were changing so fast that I felt as though I were a one-armed contestant at a greased-pig competition. I tell you, there were times that I just loaded up a battery of tests on every version of software I could find just to make sure that *something* got tested. You know where I ran those tests? I put them on the VP's new top-end machine. I don't think he even noticed the degradation in performance."

In this style, nothing is mentioned about the real problem. The audience might enjoy the digression but nothing of substance was discussed. We did not learn what the speaker really thinks *(Self)*, the problem of the configuration management system was not raised *(Context)*, and the listeners were not invited to discuss or think about the problem *(Other)*.

Applied to Retrospectives

Most of the time, people deliver congruent messages, but we all deliver incongruent messages occasionally—it's part of being human. We do this when we are under stress or when we feel vulnerable.

Because the experience of a failed project and the ensuing retrospective discussion can cause people to lose self-confidence and self-esteem, they may well offer incongruent messages during the various exercises. As facilitator, you need to recognize incongruent messages and help the message author understand the reasons for them. The first step is to help the individual achieve a higher level of self-esteem. This is tricky to bring about, especially if you are attempting to do so in front of peers. Being successful in this endeavor depends on

- the kind of relationship you have built with the person
- the information you know about the person (such as, accomplishments, yearnings, goals) and an assessment of how others see him or her
- the type of incongruent style he or she has chosen
- the topic under discussion

As stated above, my first goal always is to help people reestablish their confidence and self-esteem. I then encourage them to develop a different way of saying exactly the same thing that includes *Self, Other,* and *Context.* The best way to do this varies with each person and with the facilitator's skills, but I find that the following approaches often help to reopen communication channels.

For blamers: A place to begin is to let blamers know that they have been heard. Early in the dialogue, communicate that you are listening to what they are saying, stating that you do not necessarily agree but that you do understand. These people are usually concerned with loss of control. As they discover that someone is listening to them, a sense of control returns and their desire to blame tends to dissipate. The next step is to help them readdress the topic, focusing on the three components of *Self, Other,* and *Context.*

For placaters: Placaters may fear exposing their sense of themselves, or may not even be sure that it is okay for *Self* to exist. Begin a dialogue by delving deeper into the message, and conclude by asking, "What would you like to see happen if you could change the situation?"

For super-reasonables: People who have cut off awareness of themselves or of anyone else are harder to bring back into the present because they have isolated their feelings. As a first step, I try placing my hand gently on a super-reasonable person's forearm or shoulder. The touch usually startles the person slightly and helps me connect with him or her in order to begin exploring true feelings about the situation from the *Self* point of view. This experience can lead to a discussion about *Other,* and then to a revision of the message in terms of *Context.*

For irrelevant folk: These people want to avoid the situation completely, and attempt to derail the discussion, taking it someplace other than where it needs to go. Try to follow their tangent and, rather than returning immediately to the topic, see whether you can add to the digression. Make it a fun break for a bit, and then find a way to use what has happened as a metaphor for the real issue. Explore the metaphor and then ask how this relates to the topic at hand.

The Incongruent Facilitator

Observing incongruence in others is much easier than observing it in yourself. This fact is important to acknowledge because situations may occur in a retrospective that lower the facilitator's own self-esteem or confidence. I make a point of frequently addressing how I feel and, if I find myself being incongruent, I take a few moments to get back on track. Some steps that work for me include

- *deep breathing,* which helps me refocus my attention.
- *relaxing tense muscles,* which requires me to take a moment to notice tension in my body.
- *reviewing past events,* which compels me to ask myself, "Why am I like this? What triggered my incongruence? What am I saying to myself about how I'm leading this retrospective?"

- *reframing,* which challenges me to look for an alternate way of thinking about what just happened. I try to imagine how I would look at the situation if I had high self-esteem and great confidence and I hold onto that image in my mind.
- *laughing,* which allows me to take a moment to enjoy the fact that I'm human. I remind myself not to take matters so seriously, and give myself permission to be less than perfect.
- *making amends,* which I do when I can find a way to apologize and share what I want people to know about why I'm being incongruent. I then tell everyone that I'm going to try to rephrase the message.

The concept of congruent and incongruent messages is not an easy topic to grasp, nor is it easy to learn to work with. However, once you have mastered it, you'll have an excellent tool for assuring that retrospectives stay on track.

References for Further Reading

Satir, Virginia. *The New Peoplemaking*. Palo Alto, Calif.: Science and Behavior Books, 1988.

> This very readable book explores aspects of how people interact. I recommend that retrospective facilitators study the entire book, but point all readers to the discussion of congruence and incongruence in Chapters 7 and 8.

Weinberg, Gerald M. *Quality Software Management, Vol. 3: Congruent Action*. New York: Dorset House Publishing, 1994.

> A major proponent of the idea that, since software is built by people, developers need to understand how people work together in order to build complex systems, Weinberg drives home his point in a book that is equally valuable to retrospective facilitators and software engineers. *Volume 3* applies Satir's models of congruence and incongruence to our common software development practices.

CHAPTER TEN

After the Retrospective

Flying in from the West, Bee spotted Owl in his tree and settled on a branch near him. He wanted to talk to Owl about the Busy Bee Realty Company, which had grown so large Bee now had eighteen critters working for him. Bee began his conversation by telling Owl that much of the company's success was due to Owl's idea of holding retrospectives, and reported that he was scheduling reviews after every sale.

Pleased at Bee's news, Owl asked about Bee's staff. "I hear Singed-Tail started to work for you recently. He had such a bad time hunting that I'm glad to know he's trying something new. How's he doing?"

"He's doing a fine job!" Bee buzzed happily. "I would never have guessed he'd succeed, but he's my best sales-critter, breaking all records. Not only that, he writes newsletters and gives a seminar called 'How to Sell It All: Lairs, Dens, Tunnels, Nests, Holes, and Perches.' I guess he was born to sell."

Owl shifted a bit on his branch. "Actually, the truth is, I've coached Singed-Tail a bit. He came to me just after you hired him, worried that he didn't know anything about selling real estate. I told him to gather wisdom where he could. Right away, he started reading the reports from all your retrospectives."

Bee hesitated for a second, looking somewhat confused. "Gee, I thought those reports were private."

Owl flapped his wings and sputtered with exasperation, "Wisdom serves best when it's shared. I told Singed-Tail that, too. That's why he's writing newsletters and teaching, putting your retrospective reports into practice. He wants your wisdom to live on!"

Bee squirmed, still looking mystified, "I wonder how he got the reports?"

"He just asked for them—but while sporting a big grin," replied Owl. "When a wolf grins, he is likely to get anything he wants!"

Whether an organization develops an ongoing practice of holding retrospectives depends on what happens after its first one. If the ideas and energy that emerge during the retrospective get swallowed by the day-to-day operations of the next project, project members will have less interest in holding another retrospective. On the other hand, if the retrospective marks the beginning of a sustained attempt at serious, committed improvement of the software development process, then retrospectives will become habitual—and they will surely prove to be the most heavily relied-upon tool employed as management, project members, developers, and facilitators work together to build ever-stronger corporate units.

At the end of a retrospective, I like to select three or four action items that all members of the retrospective agree should be implemented on the next project (for example, accepted proposals from the "Cross-Affinity Teams" Exercise). More than four action items tends to be too many to expect participants to accomplish on the very next project, but a facilitator should work with the participants to identify which additional changes individuals can implement for themselves and which changes can be left to be undertaken "next time." Using input from retrospective participants, we devise a plan for the community to use to track the changes, so they are not diluted or forgotten. I also lend strong support to making a report entitled "Progress on Retrospective Action Items" a standard item to be discussed during the community's project status meetings.

As the retrospective ends, your responsibility to the particular community is nearing completion, but you may be able to take on other roles. If the community has come to appreciate your skills as a facilitator and as a leader, and if its members have become comfortable with you as part of their team, the possibilities for follow-up consulting work are good. However, whether or not you are invited to continue to work with the community, do follow up with it at various intervals to see how team members and management are progressing with their plans for change. I use both phone calls and e-mail to keep in touch with specific individuals charged with leading the changes. Usually, I contact them a couple of weeks after the retrospective to ask how they are doing and to determine whether there are small problems I can help them with. Because I do this as a follow-up to the completed retrospective on my own initiative, I charge no additional fee. However, if a true consulting assignment emerges, I let everyone know my terms so there is no confusion about the cost of ongoing work. If I am to continue to track the changes as a retrospective follow-up, I ask how often people want to hear from me.

Immediately after a retrospective, I make notes about the people I met and my impressions of them. I record who showed interest in which important issues. If feasible, I use instant-camera photographs to connect names with faces, and I flag the names of any individuals I want to stay in touch with through their subsequent projects.

RETROSPECTIVE REPORTS

The final task to be completed by participants during the retrospective is preparation of a written report that contains all pertinent details and all action items. In my early days as a facilitator, sometimes my client would ask me to write the report. I would take about a week to develop it, only to learn later that no one really made use of it! It was common for community members to ignore the report, in part because they had invested nothing in developing it. I also found that the report could be taken out of context by people who were not at the retrospective, in order to further an agenda that had nothing to do with topics discussed during the review. I now make report writing the team's final responsibility.

As a retrospective is not an event in which a facilitator evaluates the community's work, the report should be written not by the facilitator but by a committee made up of cross-affinity team members. This ensures good representation and widespread ownership. The report authors should identify their primary and secondary audiences and design the report for them. In addition to retrospective participants—the primary audience—a secondary audience might include

- upper-level managers of the specific project who were not at the retrospective

- managers of other projects who want to learn from the team's experience
- managers of subsequent projects who want to validate their own scheduling estimates by looking at historical data
- new team members added to the development staff at a later date who want to understand the history and operational norms of the group
- software-engineering process-improvement investigators

Although there is no fixed report format for a team to use, the following two pages present a sample to get the writers started. This sample is intended as a boilerplate to be modified for a particular audience.

Make sure that the report is sent to all the participants as well as to the intended readership. Most likely, the majority of participants will file the report without reading it. They were there and remember more than the report can discuss. However, a few years later, they may find the report useful as a reminder of specific details of the project.

COLLECTING RETROSPECTIVE REPORTS

I have no doubt that were the fable at the start of this chapter to be continued, we would learn that Singed-Tail missed a few reports as he pawed and sniffed through the Busy Bee Realty Company's files in search of retrospective reports. The practice of keeping a well-organized collection of retrospective reports is one of the most valuable habits a learning organization can establish, and the best way to establish the practice first involves identifying a person or group to be responsible for the collection, and then allocating a secure location to house it. In companies that are large enough to have a software-engineering process group charged with improving the firm's software-development maturity level, it's natural for these groups not only to collect the retrospective reports, but also to be trained to serve as in-house retrospective facilitators.

SAMPLE REPORT FORMAT

Section Name	Section Contents

Title page

- Name of project
- Date and location of the retrospective
- Names of the report authors
- Company confidentiality statement

Executive overview

- In a one-sentence statement, describe the goals of the retrospective (for example, a goal may have been to learn from our experiences, to repair damaged relationships, to capture effort data, to assess progress on process improvement initiatives, or some similar goal or goals).
- In one paragraph, describe what community members found that they did well.
- In one paragraph, list the three or four most important recommended changes, and then tell what the expected impact will be and who will be furthering those efforts.

Introduction

- Prepare a brief statement summarizing the project.

Effort data

- Provide details about the following: How long did the project take? How many people were involved, over what periods of time? What was the cost of the project? How many defects were discovered? How many defects were repaired?
- Compare cost and schedule estimates to actual results.

What worked well?

- From the "Develop a Time Line" Exercise, list what was recorded on the flip chart, adding any special annotations that you want to include for your intended audience.

Section Name (continued)	Section Contents (continued)
Lessons learned?	
	■ Again from the "Develop a Time Line" Exercise, record the flip-chart messages.
What to do differently next time?	
	■ Also from the "Develop a Time Line" Exercise, add additional comments to the few words captured on the flip chart.
What still puzzles us?	
	■ List the issues, and briefly discuss the importance and implications of unresolved matters. ■ Discuss how to proceed with resolving whatever puzzles are most important.
Recommendations to management	
	■ All of the cross-affinity teams wrote up their analyses and recommendations during the retrospective. Include their write-ups here.
Time-line summary	
	■ Capture the highlights of the time line, perhaps by using photographs of the time line itself or by drawings and diagrams prepared using CAD tools to show a representation of the time line. (The goal here is to create a trigger device to aid in remembering what happened during the project for those who were involved. Don't recreate all the items on the time line; identify only the most significant events.)
Participants	
	■ Record who was involved with the review. Each of the participants possesses greater knowledge than can be captured in this document, and someone may want to ask questions of them at some point in the future.

255

If a firm has no established process-improvement group, then other recommended selections include an executive such as the VP of Information Technology, whose office can be used to house the collection, or the firm's librarian, whose location and curatorial skills may be almost as valuable as the collection itself!

In searching for the perfect person and place, be certain that the person responsible will keep the information alive, and that the location is secure enough to preserve any desired degree of confidentiality. Retrospective reports that end up in a locked file cabinet will never be put to good use.

KEEPING THE WISDOM ALIVE

Singed-Tail not only collected and read retrospective reports; he kept that wisdom alive through his newsletters and his seminar. As in the story of the now-successful wolf, the group or person responsible for the collection of retrospective reports needs to package, market, *and* sell them to all possible customers. By *customers,* I especially mean project managers and technical leaders, particularly those who have just moved into leadership positions.

To keep the wisdom alive, the responsible party needs to *package* it. This means to comb through the reports, cull interesting details pertaining to the various retrospectives, analyze and summarize the information, and then post or publish it where targeted customers will see it—such as on a bulletin board located in a common area or in a regular column in a company newsletter. Trends, new ideas, and cost comparisons are just some of the topics that can be presented.

The *market* and *sell* steps also require extensive ongoing effort on the part of the retrospective collector. By proactively meeting with people who are initiating new projects and exploring with them how the collection of retrospective wisdom can assist in their planning process, the collector ensures that valuable lessons do not fade from view.

A True Story

I worked as part of a software-engineering process group when I first began facilitating. As part of our offered services, we conducted retrospectives and archived the reports. Fairly quickly, the collection of reports grew, and we discovered that the accumulated effort data became a great resource against which project managers and developers could measure whether our marketing department's dictated delivery schedules were realistic.

Experimenting with projections derived from the accumulated effort data, several of the groups we served shifted responsibility for scheduling from marketing to the programmers and developers. The results of the experimental shift were perhaps predictable but nevertheless heartening: Although marketing-dictated schedules were never met, programmer-generated schedules invariably were more accurate.

The report collection's value as a research resource was enhanced further when we were able to use the reports to identify configuration-management strategies and other improvements that had not been made operational because no one in the firm knew how to initiate them. Citing this quantitative data, we were able to justify the cost of hiring outside trainers to provide organization-wide courses, among other steps. The reports also helped us determine what courses we should develop in-house, what colloquium topics we should recommend for further discussion, and what standards efforts we needed to mandate.

Our software-engineering support group became recognized as project historians and data experts, consulted, for example, on how the firm developed software and what process improvement measures needed to be made. Knowing that we had cost data from which to develop return-on-investment calculations, managers and developers with new ideas asked us to help them with their project and process-improvement proposals. Over time, the number of retrospective reports in our archive grew to 86, providing to the firm an impressively large body of information. It was said that the value of that collection's wisdom was many times greater than its weight in gold!

Eventually, I left the group to work at another location. Because no one else had my desire to package, market, and sell retrospective wisdom, the collection of retrospective reports remained dormant and unused, filed in a cabinet. The software-engineering support group I had left continued to work together, but gradually lost its edge, failing to keep up with current soft-ware-development practices. Major software projects failed, and the firm downsized, disbanding the group.

By the time word of the group's fate had reached me, I had long since become a consultant, working to facilitate retrospectives. Suspecting that no one within my old firm cared about the 86 reports, I asked a company executive whether I could have them. He responded, "Sure—if you can find them."

Mindful of the enormity of the task, I felt jubilant when I traced the whereabouts of the old file cabinet, only to despair at finding none of the reports in it. It seemed the cabinet's current owner had needed the space, and had recycled all the "junk" that had been in the drawers.

As this is a true story, I will admit that I went out to the parking lot, climbed into my car, and shed some tears. I still cared for that company even though I was no longer an employee, but I felt most distressed that my former managers had failed to recognize and utilize a key that could have helped them solve many of their software development problems.

A Secure Location

Retrospective reports tell the real story behind the software development process used by a firm—what works, what doesn't work, and what is still puzzling. While my inclination generally is to share what we have discovered, some of my clients consider details of their software practices to be strictly confidential. They do all they can to ensure that their competition knows nothing about which tools, methodologies, technologies, or consultants they favor, or whether they have achieved results that are software successes or failures. Such firms want to be certain that information gathered in a retrospective does not become available to their competitors. Their need for security goes counter to conventional practice in which collaborators share and spread retrospective wisdom, and results in predictable conflict between differing viewpoints. Whenever I have encountered this need for complete security of information, I have worked to find a solution, always emphasizing the belief that shared information contributes to software process improvement. It takes time, energy, and lots of dialogue to build the trust necessary to release information. I use a statement such as the following to explain my conviction to advocates of nondisclosure:

> "This information is crucial for top management. It will be used only for executive summaries and as background material for decision-makers. Our goal is to justify new initiatives for software improvement, and the quantitative data we release for the justification can be limited to a small circle of executives."

I also try to encourage security-conscious people to participate in the retrospective process—perhaps by facilitating retrospectives designed to help them understand breaches in security. In the best of cases, the collection of retrospective reports becomes familiar, and security is relaxed. In the worst, I shy away from future business.

CONDUCT A RETROSPECTIVE OF YOUR RETROSPECTIVE

There is no single correct way to lead a retrospective. Retrospectives are not just intended to be used for reviewing software development projects. One can be performed to analyze just about any kind of project imaginable, including the retrospective you just facilitated.

Although we all know we can learn from our experiences in order to acquire wisdom, it's easy to "forget" to review our own performance. However, holding a review of the just-completed retrospective is the best way I know to become a better facilitator.

Therefore, after each retrospective, I meet with a few members of the community, perhaps for dinner or in the car as we drive back home. People I invite to my retrospective-of-a-retrospective usually include sponsors such as the manager who contacted me, retrospective facilitator trainees, and any others who might have a unique perspective (such as a person who hung around after the retrospective to help clean up). They all usually have something meaningful to say.

I start the discussion by rephrasing the Prime Directive: "I did the best job I could, given what I knew at the time, and I hope I learned from this experience." I say this for my own benefit as well as for that of the people giving me feedback. I then say I'd like to hear from each of them in response to a tailored set of the five questions from the "Mining the Time Line for Gold" activity:

- What worked well?
- What did you learn about leading retrospectives?
- What would you do differently next time?
- What still puzzles you about leading retrospectives?
- What skills, knowledge, and experiences do you need to acquire before we hold another retrospective?

As the now-ex-facilitator, my main job is to listen, although I do need to start the discussion by asking the five questions. During the discussion, I take notes and perhaps ask for clarification, but I resist any inclination to respond and defend my actions. If I say anything in defense or explanation, the free-flowing feedback will cease. I just take notes and thank each person for giving me input. A few days later, after a bit of rest, I return to my notes and decide how to interpret and use the feedback.

COLLECTING RETROSPECTIVES-OF-RETROSPECTIVES REPORTS

Early in this chapter, I stated my belief that there is great value in amassing a collection of retrospective reports. If such a collection is valuable, then logic suggests that a collection of retrospectives-of-retrospectives is valuable as well. To see whether this logic holds, I've established a collection of these reports on my Website (http://www.retrospectives.com).

If you acquire wisdom from leading retrospectives and can share it, please visit my Website to post your discoveries and to download others. My goal is to create a community of retrospective facilitators who will work together to improve our software profession. Please join me.

Index